Why Brazil?

Pursuing Freedom in the Americas

Why Brazil?

Pursuing Freedom in the Americas

Lucas Berlanza

&

Alex Catharino

Translated from Portuguese by Helena Mussoi

ACTON INSTITUTE

Why Brazil? Pursuing Freedom in the Americas

© 2025 by Acton Institute

All rights reserved. No part of this publication may be reproduced, stored in a retrieval system, or transmitted in any form or by any means, including elec-tronic, mechanical, photocopying, recording, or otherwise, without the prior permission of the publisher.

ISBN 979-8-218-70064-5 (paperback)

ISBN 979-8-218-69946-8 (ebook)

Acton Institute

98 E. Fulton

Grand Rapids, Michigan 49503

616.454.3080

www.acton.org

Contents

Foreword	v
Introduction	1
1. The British and Portuguese Monarchies	19
2. Portuguese America and the English Colonies	45
3. Two Liberal Processes of Independence	78
4. Crowned Liberalism and Republican Revolution	103
Conclusion	131

Foreword

The United States and Brazil possess interesting similarities. They are geographically similar in size and also the most populous countries on their respective continents. Brazil's population of over 212 million people, which has earned it the nickname of the "Nigeria of South America," means there are nearly as many Portuguese speakers as there are Spanish speakers in South America.

Lucas Berlanza and Alex Catharino argue that these two New World giants are poised to collaborate in the promotion of ordered liberty because each share so deeply in the Christian heritage of the West.

Each country has made mistakes, of course, most notably engaging in the sin of slavery. Unfortunately, this makes Brazil and the United States normative in human history, not distinctive. As it turns out, however, slavery was criticized and then outlawed in each country thanks to the argument that every person possesses an intrinsic dignity because he or she is created in the image and likeness of God. In order to make this claim, Americans drew on the Protestant tradition and Brazilians drew on Catholic Social Teaching. Yet each also argued for human freedom in a way so compatible with natural law principles that a liberal republic with freedom of religion could accept it.

The United States early on aspired to overcome what Paul Johnson calls its "original sin" in order to be a republic that could be a beacon of light and freedom to the world. Unlike the Brazilians, however, Americans possessed and then built upon a tradition of self-government and a culture of liberty.

The authors' comparison of Brazil and the United States of America shows us the important distinction between merely having a constitution and possessing a constitutional culture with deep roots in history and tradition.

Since its independence, the United States has had two constitutions. The first, the Articles of Confederation, lasted less than seven years. The second, the U.S. Constitution, was ratified in 1788.

Brazil, on the other hand, has had seven constitutions. One of these was passed in 1937 to cement the autocratic rule of the Vargas regime, another was passed in the wake of World War II to bring that regime to an end. Yet another instituted military rule in 1967 following a coup three years earlier. The current Brazilian constitution dates to 1988. The struggle for constitutionalism in Brazil continues.

Catharino and Berlanza remain hopeful for Brazil. They encourage their readers to look at what the United States and Brazil have in common, especially factors that are worthy of emulation as long as Edmund Burke's wisdom on the organic nature of society and political culture is heeded. They clearly think, however, that Brazilians have much to learn from the United States, particularly as Brazil teeters between being a free, prosperous society and degenerating into economic stagnation at the hands of illiberal statism.

Now is the time for the citizens of Brazil and the United States to learn from each other and work together for a rightly ordered liberty that promotes human dignity, encourages entrepreneurship, and produces genuine human flourishing.

—John C. Pinheiro
Director of Research
Acton Institute

Introduction

Most of the citizens in the United States, including people with an elevated degree of knowledge of other nations' politics, economy, and culture, are clearly devoid of a broad understanding regarding Brazil. Even though it was, in 2023, the ninth largest economy in the world, with a GDP of 2.3 trillion dollars; possessed, with 3,287,956.2 square miles, the third largest territory within the Americas and the fifth largest on the planet, behind only Russia, Canada, China, and the United States; and contained a population hovering around 215.3 people, the continental South American Lusophone country, surrounded by Hispanic nations, tends to be seen through a stereotypical lens, one that is widely broadcast not only by foreign media but also by Brazilians themselves, including governmental authorities.

In the popular animated sitcom *The Simpsons*, created by Matt Groening for Fox television network, the episodes "Blame it on Lisa" and "You Don't Have to Live Like a Referee", respectively the thirteenth episode of the 2003 season and the sixteenth episode of the 2013 season, have Brazil as the stories' main scenario. Both narratives depict the country as though it had wild animals roaming on the streets of big cities, within a highly corrupt and violent environment, packed with poor children, who are entertained by kids' shows presented by highly sexualized, half-naked female presenters, and with seductive adults inebriated by soccer and Carnaval dances. Unfortunately, such a caricature does not stray far from the propaganda made abroad by left-wing politicians and certain governmental organs, as well as NGOs, which are provided for by the lucrative business of poverty.

While this negative portrait has been exaggerated in the sitcom for the purpose of comedy and presented by NGOs or the government in order to get potential "clients" to take money out of their pockets, it does reflect some of the country's actual problems. Based on 2023 data from eight different indexes, the comparison between the positions occupied by Brazil and the United States offers quantitative parameters for a better comprehension of the abysmal disparities between both nations.

In accordance with the HDI (Human Development Index) presented by the UNDP (United Nations Development Program), the Brazilian and American populations fill, respectively, the 89th and 22nd positions out of all the countries in the world. When it comes to the poverty index, data provided by the World Bank shows that, in Brazil, around 19 percent of the people subsist with a daily income that is lower than 6.95 dollars, whereas, in the US, a mere 1 percent lives under those conditions. Regarding the education index, according to UNESCO (United Nations Educational,

Scientific and Cultural Organization), Brazilians and Americans are ranked 82nd and 12th, in that order. Per the Global Organized Crime Index, Brazil comes in 22nd, while the US places 67th. The statistics provided by the Intentional Homicide Rate, elaborated by the UNODC (United Nations Office on Drugs and Crime), put the South American nation in 18th, with an average of 21.3 annual homicides for every ten thousand inhabitants, while the North American nation comes in 55th, with an average of 6.4 homicides annually for every hundred thousand inhabitants. According to an inquiry produced by Corruption Perception Index, of Transparency International, the nations occupy, respectively, the 104th and 24th positions. According to the Property Rights Alliance's (PRA) International Property Rights Index (IPRI), Brazil occupies the 83rd position overall, ranking 65th in Legal and Political Environment (LP), 101st in Physical Property Rights (PPR), and 83rd in Intellectual Property Rights (IPR); whereas the United States ranks 14th (IPRI), 29th (LP), 14th (PPR), and 1st (IPR). Finally, as reported by the Index of Economic Freedom released by Heritage Foundation, being ranked 124th, Brazil falls into the category of "mostly unfree," whereas the United States is classified as "mostly free".

The reader may come to the conclusion that, given these pieces of information, the major differences between Brazil and the United States make it impossible for the two countries to integrate. Nonetheless, as we intend to demonstrate in this book's four chapters, not only do both nations share the same Judeo-Christian and European civilizational roots, but they have also had, throughout their specific historical developments, confluence points that allow for a broader interaction between those who wish to promote, both within the Brazilian environment and the American context, a free, virtuous, thriving society.

Recent events in Brazil highlight the importance of the United States as a role model for all Brazilians who fight for liberty. In the American case, the First Amendment to the Constitution, aside from assuring religious freedom and establishing separation of church and state, also grants freedom of speech and freedom of press to all citizens. Even though Paragraph IV in Article 5 of the current Brazilian Constitution, promulgated in 1988, affirms that "the expression of thought is free, anonymity being forbidden," the actions taken by certain judicial authorities seem to contradict the constitutional rights that have been established. Within the context of the COVID-19 pandemic, under the pretext of avoiding the spread of "fake new" and containing "hate speech," the Brazilian Supreme Court (*Supremo Tribunal Federal*, STF) set up an illegal inquiry which, in practice, has been over the past five years serving the purpose of implementing a sort of censorship in disguise.

The result of such arbitrary measures, taken by those who should be acting as guardians of the law, is a general dread among many Brazilians toward freely expressing their ideas. A survey released by *Veja* magazine in May 2024 found that 61 percent of Brazilians fear the possibility of being punished for speaking or writing what they think, whereas those who believe they can express themselves without reprisals represent a mere 32.4 percent of the population (6.6 percent couldn't or wouldn't issue an opinion on the matter). The denouncement of the Brazilian situation issued by American journalist Michael Shellenberger in the "Twitter Files" case—aside from the controversial report made by Elon Musk upon questioning Brazilian authorities on the censorship practices nationwide—shows the severity of the problem.[1] The circumstances in Brazil have taken on proportions that led the Tom Lantos Human Rights Commission (TLHRC) of the United States House of Representatives, following several hearings with Brazilian parliamentarians and journalists, to induce the Inter-American Commission of Human Rights (IACHR) to issue a request for information on the grave allegations of violation of human rights in the South American country. The role of the United States in the fight by some Brazilians in favor of freedom, however, goes far beyond measures such as this.

Having acted as a Brazilian representative on cultural action commissions of the Organization of American States (OAS) and for social development in the United Nations (UN) in the 1950s and 1960s, lawyer, journalist, and literary scholar Clodomir Vianna Moog (1906–1988) wrote a book comparing the *bandeirantes*

---

1. Using Twitter's internal documentation, Shellenberger found, for example, that an STF justice "demanded access to Twitter's internal data, in violation of Twitter policy," and "sought to censor, unilaterally, Twitter posts by sitting members of Congress." *Rio Times*, April 5, 2024.

of Brazil with the "pioneers" of the United States, a topic that shall be more thoroughly discussed in the second chapter of this volume. Originally released in 1954 in Portuguese, his work was published in English in 1964, and it remains a fundamental study for understanding the main cultural differences between the two nations, as well as a warning on the paths Brazilians should follow in order to achieve a degree of prosperity that is similar to that Americans have built through their hard labor.[2]

Some other crucial works written by Brazilian authors have also been translated into English. Among such works, the most noteworthy are the writings of sociologist, historian, anthropologist, literary scholar, painter, journalist, and parliamentarian Gilberto Freyre (1900–1987), one of the most prominent Brazilian thinkers of the twentieth century. Freyre attended Baylor University and Columbia University, and was heavily influenced by German-American sociologist Franz Boas (1858–1942), as well as by several other American authors. The most famous book by this illustrious conservative, *The Masters and the Slaves*, released for the first time in Portuguese as *Casa Grande e Senzala* in 1933, was later translated into English, as were the volumes *The Mansions*

---

2. Clodomir Vianna Moog, *Bandeirantes and Pioneers* (G. Braziller, 1964). *Bandeirantes* were colonial-era settlers who played a role similar to that of American pioneers, expanding the frontier of Brazil from the sixteenth through nineteenth centuries.

and the Shanties, initially published as *Sobrados e Mucambos* in 1936, and *Order and Progress*, first published as *Ordem e Progresso* in 1959, which constitute a trilogy on the history of the Brazilian patriarchal society. Stemming from conferences held by Freyre during the fall of 1944 in Indiana State University, the book *Brazil: An Interpretation* was conceived as a summarized exposition for foreign readers of Brazilian social formation as an amalgamation of races and cultures. It was originally published in English in 1945 and posthumously in Portuguese in 1947.[3]

The study of the history of Brazil has been the object of a number of foreign researchers, known as Brazilianists, among whom American scholars are prominent. Leaving aside the countless works in the English language by Brazilian authors, from 1940 to 1969 only five works by American scholars on Brazil were published in the United States, whereas, between 1970 and 1989, the number of books written by Americans on the same topic was fifty-six, most of them focused on the Brazilian Republican epoch (1889–1930). Arguably, the most notable American Brazilianist is historian Thomas Skidmore (1932–2016), who wrote four books

---

3. Gilberto Freyre, *The Masters and the Slaves: A Study in the Development of Brazilian Civilization*, 2nd ed. (Knopf, 1956); *The Mansions and the Shanties: The Making of Modern Brazil* (Knopf, 1963); *Order and Progress: Brazil from Monarchy to Republic* (Knopf, 1970); *Brazil: An Interpretation* (Knopf, 1945).

on the continental South American country. Here it is worth highlighting historian John W. F. Dulles (1913–2008)—the eldest son of former Secretary of State John Foster Dulles (1888–1959) and brother of Catholic theologian Cardinal Avery Dulles SJ (1918–2008)—who published in English eight voluminous books on Brazil, including biographies of Presidents Getúlio Vargas (1882–1954) and Humberto Castelo Branco (1897–1967), as well as journalist and politician Carlos Lacerda (1914–1977) and jurist Heráclito Sobral Pinto (1893–1991); and important studies on the anarchist communist movements in Brazil, from 1900 to 1935, and on the repression of communism in the nation, from 1935 to 1945. Other important names among American Brazilianists are sociologist Donald Pierson (1900–1955), economist Werner Baer (1931–2016), literary critic Helen Caldwell (1904–1987), and historians Alexander Marchant (1912–1981), Stanley J. Stein (1920–2019), Warren Dean (1932–1994), Neill W. Macaulay Jr. (1935–2007), and Frank McCann (1938–2021).

From a popular standpoint, media depictions were more influential than the studies made by the aforementioned scholars. Unlike the more recent and comical negative view presented on *The Simpsons* in 2003 and 2013, more positive portrayals can be found in the not-so-distant past. In the animated features *Saludos Amigos* (1942) and *The Three Caballeros* (1944), the Walt Disney Company presented the character José Carioca to stereotypically represent, as a happy-go-lucky and clever parrot, the figure of the Brazilian common man. In the same period, Hollywood's film studios imported the singer, dancer, and actress Carmen Miranda (1909–1955) as the representative of Brazilian culture to the American audience. The United States was at the time striving, in the midst of World War II, to cultivate a "policy of good neighborliness," seeking to strengthen bonds with Brazil through these kinds of symbolic advances.

The result was quite positive, seeing that, due to the diplomatic efforts and financial incentives of the United States, along with popular pressure exerted by Brazilians, dictator Getúlio Vargas, despite having displayed sympathy toward the Axis powers, militarily aligned Brazil with the Allies. He allowed the installment of American military bases and sent a Brazilian Expeditionary Force (*Força Expedicionária Brasileira*, FEB), constituted by nearly 25,900 Brazilian soldiers, to fight in the Italian campaign from July 1944 until the end of the conflict. The FEB ended up serving as the US Fifth Army division in the 15th Army Group.[4]

Following the end of the worldwide conflict, a great cultural influx from the United States to Brazil occurred. In lieu of the hegemonic French influences that had marked the Brazilian environment throughout the whole nineteenth and the beginning of the twentieth centuries, most Brazilians started consuming a

---

4. Further information on Brazilian participation in the conflict, especially regarding the nation's support of the US, can be found in Frank McCann, *Brazil and the United States During World War II and Its Aftermath: Negotiating Alliance and Balancing Giants* (Palgrave MacMillan, 2018).

variety of North American products. It is an undeniable fact that the Brazilian urban contemporary context has constantly received, as it still does, a great cultural influence from the United States, especially via the entertainment industry—cinema, music, and sports—but also through several American franchises and branches of American factories present in the country.

There is an extensive connection between Brazil and the United States, so that, both in economic activities and in cultural terms, Brazilians are closer to North Americans than they are to their Hispanic neighbors. Nor is the relationship between the two nations a one-way street. Aside from popular music—especially the bossa nova of composer, pianist, and singer Antônio Carlos Jobim (1927–1994), whose magnificent compositions have fascinated American stars such as Ella Fitzgerald (1917–1996) and Frank Sinatra (1915–1998)—there is the popularity of Edson Arantes do Nascimento (1940–2022), widely known by the nickname Pelé, and several other soccer superstars.

There is also a vigorous trading relationship between the two countries. According to the most recent published report (2023) by Amcham Brasil, Brazilian representative in the US Chamber of Commerce, the bilateral trading market of goods between the nations was $88.7 billion in 2022, surpassing by 25.8 percent the historical mark of the previous year. Seeing an increase of 30.3 percent in comparison to 2021, Brazilian imports from the US reached the milestone of $51.3 billion, while exports from Brazil to the American market reached the never-before-seen mark of $37.4 billion dollars, growth of 20.2 percent, resulting in a trade surplus of $13.9 billion dollars for the US. In 2022, US participation represented 14.6 percent of the total flow of Brazilian commerce. Surpassed only by the trading of merchandise with China, with a flow of 22.3 percent, American products represent 18.8 percent of the tax flow in Brazil, while, also in the second position, the US is responsible for 11.2 percent of Brazilian exports. The most valuable exported products from Brazil to the US are (1) crude petroleum oils, (2) semi-finished products of iron and steel, (3) aircraft, (4) pig iron, (5) unroasted coffee, (6) civil engineering equipment, (7) cellulose, (8) wood products, (9) construction materials, and (10) fruit and vegetables.

The data presented above demonstrate the importance, to both Brazil and the US, of the two-way trade between the nations. There is great potential in this relationship, and there are vast resources to be utilized within both countries. Solid economic forecasts predict continued growth in the relations between Americans and Brazilians. As the largest South American economic power, Brazil is not merely an exporter of raw materials; the United States imports an ever-increasing amount of Brazilian manufactured products, notably Embraer aircraft, which serve a significant portion of American regional air routes. It is worth noting, too, the importance of the US in the process of industrialization in Brazil. The establishment in 1941 of the National Steel Company (*Companhia Siderúrgica Nacional*), to provide steel for the Allies during World War II, was one of the key outcomes of the agreement made between the Brazilian and American governments.

All of this notwithstanding, one must stress that there is a problem rooted in the Brazilian industrialization process, as it was artificially conducted by an authoritarian and interventionist government, which made the sector highly dependent on state aid. The most notorious Brazilian controversy in respect to economic planning was the debate, between August 1944 and August 1945, in the federal government's Economic Planning Commission. On one side was the engineer, industrialist, parliamentarian, and economist Roberto Simonsen (1889–1948), who argued for developmental assistance and state intervention as a means to industrialize the country. On the other was the engineer and economist Eugênio Gudin (1886–1986), a great advocate of free markets, who stressed the importance of agriculture for the Brazilian economy and the need for the industrialization process to be led by private entrepreneurs rather than governmental bureaucrats.[5] It is noteworthy that this classical liberal Brazilian economist also took part in the Bretton Woods Conference, at which, in opposition to the ideas of John Maynard Keynes (1883–1946), he supported the monetary concepts proposed by Austrian economist Ludwig von Mises (1881–1973). Besides being the first Brazilian member of Mont Pèlerin Society, Gudin held office as Minister of Finance in

---

5. The documents elaborated by both economists in the confrontation were collected and published in Roberto Simonsen and Eugênio Gudin, *A Controvérsia do Planejamento na Economia Brasileira*, 3rd ed. (Ipea, 2010).

the short period between September 1954 and April 1955, during the presidency of João Café Filho (1899–1970), during which he sought to implement an agenda of economic stability and a free market.

After eight decades, the issues discussed in the 1940s controversy remain current in Brazil, not only within the theoretical sphere but especially in conceptions regarding the role of the state in the economy that guide a substantial portion of politicians and entrepreneurs and in the current results of the so-called real economy. One might say that Roberto Simonsen's ideas have been victorious, as they conquered the minds of almost all politicians and businessmen, who benefit from state subsidies or governmental regulation of economic sectors. Nonetheless, the economic reality of Brazilian agribusiness, especially concerning the production of grain and livestock, shows that Eugênio Gudin's analysis was correct.

Unlike what occurs in most countries, where agriculture is largely dependent on governmental subsidies and state protectionism, agribusiness in Brazil is a role model for the world of entrepreneurship and economic freedom. While, during the late 1970s there was in Brazil a high degree of dependency on food imports, the situation has changed quite a bit over the last few decades. Brazil now stands out on the world stage as a leader in agricultural production and global food security. According to a report released in February 2023 by the Institute of Applied Economic Research (*Instituto de Pesquisa Econômica Aplicada*), in 2022, with 16.4 percent of its value as exports, Brazilian agribusiness amassed a trade surplus of $8.69 billion. According to the Food and Agriculture Organization (FAO), Brazilian agriculture took the fifth position in the global ranking in 2021, with 2.6 percent of global food production, which is worth a total of $158 billion.

Coming behind only China, the United States, and India, Brazilian agribusiness is the fourth largest commodities producer in that area, as it is responsible for 10.5 percent of the world harvest. Thanks to the combination of technology, entrepreneurs' hard labor, and favorable weather, Brazilian agriculture now produces second and third crops, which assures a unique productivity potential. The country thus assumes more and more a vocation to feed the planet, having been responsible in 2022 for 8.4 percent of worldwide market share. In a recent academic study on Brazilian agribusiness, attorney and researcher Patrícia Arantes de Paiva Medeiros discussed the stiff competition between Brazil, China, and the United States in the agricultural market. Grounding her analysis in the legal systems of all three nations and drawing on several key statistics, Medeiros suggested the following:

> The high level of competitiveness of products and the regional development boom initiated by production within Brazil's countryside are highlights of the

North American region, hence making the market even more competitive and heated.[6]

Despite being a fierce competitor of the United States within the agricultural field, as well as competing with Chinese and some European Union nations' agriculture, Brazilian agribusiness tends to be a more suitable partner to Americans than other rivals. Unlike Europe, Brazilian agriculture operates in a way that is closer to a free-market economy. Brazil's producers are not subject to extremely protectionist policies and do not receive large state subsidies as do European farmers. In Brazil, agribusiness is mainly capitalized by a competitive model of rural credit, with resources derived from the financial system, which allows producers to have access to technology and the required machinery to increase production. Contrary to what is broadcast by leftist propaganda, spread abroad by both Brazilian and international NGOs, Brazilian agriculture operates according to high environmental standards.

However, much like other private-sector economic activities nationwide, agricultural potential is frequently limited by the so-called "Brazil cost": a set of structural, bureaucratic, labor, and economic difficulties that get in the way of wealth creation. Con-

---

6. Patrícia Arantes de Paiva Medeiros, *Análise Econômica do Agronegócio: Competitividade no Mercado Agropecuário Global* (Editora CEDES, 2024), 66.

tinued advance therefore depends on government reform, a point underlined by the aforementioned research of Patrícia Medeiros. She concludes that

> Brazilian agribusiness is the main productive sector within the national economy and must be grounded in a market strategy and, first and foremost, a state policy strategy that fosters an increase in internal and international investment, thus enabling its growth and prosperity in the field.[7]

In light of the data presented so far, we believe there is a pressing need to strengthen cooperation between Brazilians and North Americans, not only with respect to economic relations but even more within the arena of intellectual combat in favor of freedom. Without a doubt, in Brazil the fallacious ideas disseminated by Karl Marx (1818–1883) and his epigones are hegemonic, and progressive and socialist ideas dominate the nation's traditional press. Aside from the great influence of leftist European thinkers, especially French and German ones, in the past, the Brazilian left-wing also feeds on the content produced by the North American left-wing in order to deploy its pernicious agendas. These days, the most rampant systemic problem within the Brazilian intellectual landscape is the so-called "woke movement," with its

---

7. Medeiros, *Análise Econômica do Agronegócio*, 165.

distorted identitarian and environmental agendas. In many cases, such projects take on anticapitalistic, anti-American, anti-Semitic, and anti-Christian shapes. In truth, what's at stake in that fight is the support of the most sacred principles of order, freedom, and justice within Western civilization—no longer threatened, as it once was, by barbaric invasions or other external powers, but rather by the corruption of its own youth, who are misled by false notions.

In one of the worst moments in recent history, when so many thought Brazil would follow the same path taken by Venezuela and descend into the oppression of socialism, millions of ordinary citizens took to the streets between 2014 and 2016 in defense of family, religion, the motherland, and freedom from corruption and communism. In those protests, it was common to see young people carrying banners or wearing T-shirts with the slogan "Less Marx, More Mises" (*Menos Marx, Mais Mises*), which shows a substantial transformation in the mentality of an increasing number of Brazilians. In 1959, the Austrian economist Ludwig von Mises delivered six lectures in Argentina, and in the last stated, "Ideas and only ideas can light the darkness. These ideas must be brought to the public in such a way that they persuade people. We must convince them that these ideas are the right ideas and not the wrong ones."[8]

---

8. Ludwig von Mises, *Economic Policy: Thoughts for Today and Tomorrow* (Liberty Fund, 2010), 75.

The path to be trod so as to prevent both the United States and Brazil from taking "the road to serfdom" is long and arduous. Undoubtedly, it is possible for Americans and Brazilians to expand their collaboration in the fight for freedom by exchanging successful experiences, learning from mistakes made in the past, and most importantly working together in certain common battles. However, in order for that to happen, a mutual discernment regarding the various points of convergence, as well as those of divergence, is called for, as is recognition of certain peculiarities within the two nations' politics and cultures. Over the next four chapters, such characteristics will be exposed. We hope that this book can bring American free-market conservatives and their Brazilian congeners closer together.

1

THE BRITISH AND PORTUGUESE MONARCHIES

Several elements of American and Brazilian politics and culture are deeply grounded in the civilizational influence of Jerusalem, Athens, and Rome, as well as in the legacy of medieval Christianity, which amalgamated the distinguished patrimonies bequeathed by those three ancient civilizations. Nonetheless, there are also numerous differences between the two nations, derived from the distinct trajectories charted by the respective monarchies of England and Portugal, in addition to the colonization models implemented by those kingdoms in their territories and the specific independence processes that produced these two great American nations. According to the narrative of the prominent conservative thinker Russell Kirk (1918–1994) presented in his monumental *The Roots of American Order*, the history of the

United Stated is a tale of five cities: Jerusalem, Athens, Rome, London, and Philadelphia.[1]

Brazilian society, much like American society, is a follower of Jewish and Christian spiritual legacies, centered in Jerusalem, which have provided the West with its moral and religious bases. Likewise, the Brazilian motherland is also heir to Greek and Roman classic traditions, which have arisen, respectively, in Athens and Rome, whose luminaries have molded both the Christian West's philosophical, moral, juridical, and historical thinking and various institutions within the European nations throughout the medieval period, including the overseas possessions those nations established in other continents in modernity. Kirk's analysis of the United States applies as well to Brazil's historical development, except that the cities of Lisbon and Rio de Janeiro, rather than London and Philadelphia were the last two important sources of Brazilian culture and politics.

Even though there are many diverging aspects of the British and Portuguese experiences, it is nonetheless possible to list some convergent points between the courts of London and Lisbon, and these go beyond the solid diplomatic, military, commercial and dynastic alliances established by the two nations. Several of these convergences have forged the current similarities between the two American nations, which have allowed the United States to exert

---

1. Russell Kirk, *The Roots of American Order*, 4th ed. (ISI Books, 2003).

a great deal of influence over not only the Brazilian mentality but also Brazilian political institutions, which will be further discussed later. The aim of this chapter is to present the most substantial differences and similarities, be it during the Middle Ages or modern times, between the historical trajectories followed by the British and Portuguese monarchies.

Among the most significant similarities between the kingdoms of Portugal and England, we may highlight six. First, both in the Iberian Peninsula and in the British Isles, the original populations were superseded by Celtic immigrants who, in turn, mingled with the indigenous peoples and other ethnicities that came later. Second, there was the long Roman rule in the provinces of Lusitania and Britannia, from 29 BC to AD 411, which, even in antiquity, made it possible for the third common aspect to emerge: the gradual process of Christianization in both regions. Fourth, both of these former Roman provinces, as well other Western European and Northern Africa areas, experienced violent invasions of German Barbarians during the collapse of the Roman Empire. The fifth similitude stems from the fact that the current British and Portuguese territories were invaded later as well. The British territories by Vikings and the Portuguese by Muslims.

Lastly, the formation of a strong monarchy in both countries, in comparison to other Western European nations, was quite late. The process of monarchical consolidation within the British context occurred throughout a period of nearly a century and a half, between 866 and 1066, from the unification of the seven Anglo-Saxon kingdoms by Alfred the Great (871–899) to the conquest of the Normans by William I (1027–1087) and his coronation as the English monarch in the same year.[2] Meanwhile, having been part of the long Christian Reconquest of the Iberian Peninsula (722–1492), occupied by Muslims since 711, Portugal's liberation from both Islamic rule and the Kingdom of León was due to Dom Afonso I (1109–1185), the first Portuguese monarch. Afonso, after defeating the Moors in the Battle of Ourique, on July 25, 1139, was acclaimed as king of Portugal by his troops, thereby establishing the Dynasty of Burgundy. His legitimacy was acknowledged both by Leonine sovereign Afonso VII (1105–1157), with his signature on October 5, 1143, in the Treaty of Zamora; and by Pope Alexander III (1105–1181), upon issuing on May 23, 1179, the bull *Manifestis Probatum*.[3]

---

2. We recommend the report made by Scottish philosopher David Hume (1711–1776) in chapters 2–4 of the first of six volumes of his monumental historical work, currently available in the following edition: David Hume, *The History of England: From the Invasion of Julius Caesar to the Revolution in 1688*, 6 vols. (Liberty Fund, 1983).

3. The most complete account of the first Portuguese monarch, unfortunately unavailable in English, is José Mattoso, *D. Afonso Henriques* (Temas e Debates, 2007). A general narrative of Portuguese history in English is António Henrique R. de Oliveira Marques, *History of Portugal*, 2 vols. (Columbia University Press, 1972).

In their parallel courses, the cities wherein the courts of both kingdoms were established played crucial roles, as they still do; even now, both capitals remain the most populous cities within their countries. Recent archeological excavations have shown traces of human occupations in the proximity of the Thames and Tagus Rivers where, respectively, London and Lisbon are located, prior to the twelfth century BC. Moreover, material remains from both sites indicate that there was great commercial activity in both areas, an element which, throughout British and Portuguese histories, has constituted one of the key factors that contributed to the elevated cultural development of the two ancient metropoles.

Understanding the general lines of the history of Lisbon is paramount for comprehension of the Portuguese monarchy and the nation's political, cultural, and economic development.[4] According to popular tradition, today's city of Lisbon was founded by the Greek mythical hero Ulysses, whereas archeological sources prove that, around the year 1200 BC, the region, especially its harbor, was used as a trading post by Phoenician navigators. The Phoenicians founded the colony of Alis Ubbo, whose name translates as "safe harbor," with the goal of securing the routes to the Isles of Scilly and Cornwall in Great Britain, where they would buy pewter. The same kind of economic activity was later maintained

---

4. A general survey of the historical development of Lisbon is Barry Hatton, *Queen of the Sea: A History of Lisbon* (C. Hurst, 2018).

by Carthaginians and Romans. Even though it wasn't the capital of Lusitania (which was instead Augusta Emerita, now Merida in Spain), the city of Olissipo, as it was then known, was between the first century BC and the fifth century AD the province's most important trading center. The subsequent lootings and invasions of Olissipo, perpetrated by Vandals, Alans, Goths, Suebi, and, finally, Visigoths, greatly weakened the city, which ended up losing its political connection to Constantinople, although preserving its trade relations with the Byzantines.

In the year 469, the city was integrated into the Suebi kingdom, whose capital was then established in Bracara Augusta, now Braga, Portugal. Under the Visigothic kingdom, with its court located in Toledo, which had unified the whole Iberian Peninsula, the former Olissipo was given the name Ulishbona. After three centuries of lootings and invasions, it had lost most of its commercial dynamism and was reduced to the condition of a mere village.

During the period of the Ummayad invasions of the Iberian Peninsula, led by Berber general Tárique ibn Ziade (670–720) from 711 onward, the village was conquered by Abdalazize ibne Muça (685–716) and named Alusbuna under Moorish rule. The city reclaimed its cultural and economic prominence, promoted not only by Shiites and Sunnis but also by Jews and Mozarabic Christians. However, the city's opulence made it a target for various invaders, and it was attacked in 844 and 966 by Viking fleets, as well as by the troops of Ordoño I (830–866) of Asturias in the middle of the ninth century, and those of Alfonso VI (1045–1109) of León and Castile in 1093. From the fragmentation of the

Caliphate of Córdoba around the year 1000 to the foundation of the Almohad Caliphate in 1111 by Ali ibne Iúçufe (1084–1143), the city's loyalty swung between the authorities in Badajoz and Seville, which enhanced its autonomy and economic development.

As a result of victory in the Battle of Ourique in 1139, Count Afonso Henriques finally took possession of the renowned Lisbon on November 1, 1147, after the Moorish city had been besieged from July 1 to October 25 of the same year, by Portuguese troops backed by crusader soldiers, catapults, towers, and ships, mostly British and Norman but also Flemish and Colognian. It is worth noting that, with the re-creation of the Diocese of Lisbon, the bishop appointed by the Portuguese monarch was the English monk Gilbert of Hastings (d. 1166), who had taken part in the Second Crusade and was consecrated by Dom João Peculiar (d. 1175), archbishop of Braga and primate of Spain, to which he had pledged his allegiance.

A royal charter issued in 1179 by King Alfonso I granted the privilege of establishing a great new fair in Lisbon, which resulted in the city recovering its former commercial prestige by drawing Christian and Jewish merchants, who brokered trade between the North and Mediterranean Seas. This also made it possible, subsequently, for the Portuguese to establish merchant houses in the Spanish city of Seville, the English city of Southampton, the Belgian city of Bruges, and dozens of other cities within the Hanseatic League, which, in turn, installed a community in Lisbon. The economic power due to commerce was responsible both for an increase in population and a cultural upspring, and, a few years after the reconquest, it became the most important Portuguese city.

Given the importance acquired by the city, the court was transferred in 1256 from Coimbra to Lisbon, along with the kingdom's archives and treasury. King Denis I (1261–1325), who founded in Lisbon in 1290 the university later moved to Coimbra, was also responsible for extensive renovations in the kingdom's capital. In the ecclesiastical sphere, the Diocese of Lisbon, by means of the pontifical bull *In Eminentissimae Dignitatis*, enacted November 10, 1393, by Pope Boniface IX (1356–1404), was elevated to the status of archdiocese; it was later made a patriarchate by the promulgation, on March 1, 1710, of the pontifical bull *Apostolatus Ministerio* by Pope Clement XI (1649–1721).

The relationships between the Portuguese court installed in Lisbon and the British court based in London constitute the most enduring diplomatic alliance in European history.[5] In the year 1373, British king Edward III (1312–1377) signed the Anglo-Portuguese Treaty with King Fernando I (1345–1383) and queen consort

---

5. The issue is discussed in both diplomatic and political aspects in Edgar Prestage, *Chapters in Anglo-Portuguese Relations* (Voss and Michael, 1935); A. B. W. Chapman and V. M. Shillinton, *Commercial Relations of England and Portugal* (Routledge, 2005); and Luci M. E. Shaw, *The Anglo-Portuguese Alliance and the English Merchants in Portugal, 1654–1810* (Ashgate, 1998).

Leonor Teles (1350–1405), the last monarchs of the Burgundy Dynasty, and this treaty assured the establishment of perpetual friendship, association, and alliance between the two maritime nations, which has been subsequently reinforced by new treaties and is still in effect.

Among the later agreements, the Treaty of Windsor deserves special mention. It was signed on May 9, 1386, by British king Richard II (1367–1400) and Portuguese ambassador Fernando Afonso de Albuquerque (1327–1387), representative of King João I (1357–1433), the first monarch of the House of Aviz. This arranged for João's marriage to the British Philippa of Lancaster (1360–1415), daughter of John of Gaunt (1340–1399), the Duke of Lancaster, and sister of future king Henry IV (1367–1413). The union between the English queen consort and the Lusitanian monarch begat the future Portuguese king Duarte I (1301–1438); the famous navigator prince Henrique (1394–1460), Duke of Viseu and founder of the famous School of Sagres; and the prince crusader Blessed Fernando (1402–1443), the "Holy Infante"; among other children.

The treaty was invoked throughout the centuries, in the War of Spanish Succession in 1702; in the Peninsular War in 1807; in World War I in 1916; in World War II in 1943; and in the Falklands War in 1982. More than a military alliance, however, the Treaty of Windsor was also responsible for the establishment of a bilateral commercial agreement through which England provided Portugal with codfish, wool, and fabric, and, in turn, the Portuguese exported wine, olive oil, cork, and salt to England.

In the contexts of the Portuguese Restoration War and the 1660 monarchic restoration in England, the bonds of friendship between the kingdoms were reinforced by the signature, in 1660 and 1661, of new treaties. In the first, between 1640 and 1663, Portugal broke free of the rule of the Spanish Crown, exerted by the House of Habsburg from 1580 to 1640. The second occurred after the disastrous period of the republican dictatorship implemented by Oliver Cromwell (1599–1658) as a result of the 1640 Civil War. Even during the outbreak of the British revolutionary process, by means of a treaty signed in 1643, King Charles I (1600–1649) supported the Portuguese dynastic restoration against the Iberian Union; he had been acknowledged by the court of Lisbon as the only legitimate British authority, contrary to the pretensions of the republicans. At the time of the restoration of the monarchy in England, besides naval support, two thousand English soldiers and five hundred horses were sent to help Portugal in its fight against the Spanish.

Nonetheless, the key factor for the strengthening of the alliance between the kingdoms during that period was the marriage in 1662 of British king Charles II (1630–1685) to Portuguese princess Catherine of Braganza (1638–1705), daughter of King João IV (1604–1656), the first monarch of the House of Braganza. Catherine was the sister of future Portuguese kings Afonso VI (1643–1683) and Pedro II (1648–1706), as well as the aunt of the future João V (1689–1750), on whose formation she exerted remarkable influence. She was unpopular in England due to being a Catholic—the reason she was never crowned—and to being accused of taking part in the fictional Popish Plot, created by perjurer Titus Oates (1649–1705). She also failed to produce an heir to the throne, which led to the ascension of James II (1633–1701). Even so, habits that became a distinguished part of the British culture, such as using cutlery during meals, consuming orange jam and marmalade, smoking tobacco, and finally, drinking tea, are owed to the English queen consort of Portuguese origin.

After Catherine's return to Lisbon, due to the increase in British anti-Catholic sentiment following the Glorious Revolution in 1688, the former queen played a critical role in the Lusitanian court. She facilitated the 1703 signing of the Treaties of Lisbon and Methuen between Portugal and England, now under the government of Queen Anne (1665–1714). By these, the kingdom of Portugal joined the Great Alliance against Spain and France, and a trade pact allowed for the import of English manufactured fabrics and the export of Portuguese wines, with customs tax rates a third lower than those set for similar products exported by other countries, which popularized the consumption of port wine among the British.

The historical development of London shares a few notable similarities with Lisbon's. The proximity of the cities to major rivers provided for the establishment of strong commercial activity in both. As the headquarters of the kingdoms of England and Portugal, the cities took the position of epicenters of cultural flowering in the two friendly nations. The cities also suffered similar tragedies: the Great Fire of London, September 2–5, 1666, and the Lisbon Earthquake on November 1, 1755, which resulted both in great human and material loss and in great urban renovations. Both cities had previously been afflicted by several lootings and invasions and by the Black Death.[6]

As with Lisbon, the knowledge of certain historical aspects of London is paramount for the historical comprehension of the English monarchy, as well as the cultural, economic, social, and political developments of British and American societies.[7] Although traces found in archeological research suggest the existence of human occupation and commercial activity between the years 4500 and 1500 BC in the area near the Thames River where the present-day city of London was built and the pseudo-historical work *Historia Regum Britanniae* by Welsh monk Geoffrey

---

6. On that topic, we suggest the following work: Gregory Zacharia, "After the Apocalypse: A Comparative Study of the Black Death, London Fire, and Lisbon Earthquake," *History Honors Projects*, 24 (2018). Available online at: https://digitalcommons.macalester.edu/history_honors/24

7. Among the countless reports on the city's history, we recommend the reading of the following work: Malcolm Billings, *London: A Companion to Its History and Archaeology* (Kyle Cathie, 1994). The Kirkian perspective on the topic can be found in: Kirk, *The Roots of American Order*, 177-183.

of Monmouth (1100–1155) affirms the existence of the mythic Kaerlud[8], one must consider the foundation of Londinium by Roman invaders, around AD 50, as the initial step of the town's urbanization process.

Since its foundation in 29 BC, even with periods of greater or lesser economic and cultural activity due to invasions and lootings, Lisbon has consistently remained a large urban center, whereas the history of London, in the time frame between its foundation by the Romans and its conquest by the Normans in 1066, has seen alternating periods of development and retraction, even to the point of its being abandoned altogether. The evacuation of the territory was directly related to the invasions and pillages of which the city was a victim during ancient times and the Middle Age, attacked by Iceni, Picts, Scots, Saxons, Frisians, Jutes, and Vikings.[9] From the year 1066 until modern times, London has never again been taken by force, despite attempts made by France, Spain, and more recently, Nazi Germany.

Even though strong commercial and diplomatic relations having been built between the courts of London and Lisbon throughout a period of over six and a half centuries and there are many

---

8. Geoffrey of Monmouth, *The History of the Kings of Britain* (The Folio Society, 1984).

9. Yet again, we recommend the elaborate narrative written by David Hume, who discusses said period of the English history in: Hume, *The History of England*, vol. 1, 3-185.

commonalities between the two kingdoms, one must stress the divergent practices in England and Portugal concerning the relationship between society and its governors. To some extent, Portuguese society's dependence on the Crown is due to the fact that the first Lusitanian monarch was the liberator of the people both from Moorish domination and vassalage under the Kingdom of León, not to mention that his successors were promoters of the maintenance of order, security, justice, and liberty, as well as being responsible for maritime expansion and the end of the Spanish rule.

Throughout the history of England, on the other hand, the monarch was frequently regarded as an outsider, as occurred with the dynasty of Normandy from 1066 to 1135, the Angevin Plantagenet dynasty between 1154 and 1399, the Welsh House of Tudor from 1485 to 1603, the Scottish House of Stuart from 1603 to 1714, and finally, the German Houses of Hanover from 1714 to 1901 and Saxe-Coburg-Gotha from 1901 to the present (the latter having in 1917, in the context of World War I, changed its to Windsor, given the anti-German sentiment of the British at the time). Beyond the fact that this characteristic of the British monarchy, within a theoretical sphere, may be considered to be one of the historical justifications for the libertarian theory of the "stationary bandit,"[10] one could add that it represents one of the factors responsible for the many animosities between the throne and the gentry and the throne and the clergy within the English political experience.

In large part, the British parliamentary tradition, as well as the United States' ideal of ordered liberty, stems from the aforementioned fact that, over various periods of English history, the monarch was regarded as an interloper who threatened the rights of his subjects. Americans' suspicion regarding the hovering menace of government usurping freedom is historically supported by the experiences in England involving the conflicts waged against the Crown's authoritarian measures.

One of the most notorious cases of such a quarrel between the throne and society in England was, without a doubt, the impo-

---

10. As opposed to the Hobbesian, Lockean, and Rousseauean social contract theories, the thesis was mainly disseminated by German anthropologist Franz Oppenheimer (1864-1943) and American economists e Murray N. Rothbard (1926-1995) and Mancur Olson (1932-1998) in the respective works: Franz Oppenheimer, *The State: Its History and Development Viewed Sociologically* (Transaction Publishers, 1999); Murray N. Rothbard, *Anatomy of the State* (Ludwig von Mises Institute, 2009); Mancur Olson, *The Logic of Collective Action: Public Goods and the Theory of Groups* (Harvard University Press, 1965).

sition on King John (1166–1216), also known as John Lackland, by the barons and the clergy, of the signature of the Magna Carta on July 15, 1215, which became not only a significant legal landmark for the guarantee of concrete liberties, but also an important element in the theoretical framework of supporters of individual rights.[11] One should recall, moreover, that, aside from the Civil War waged between 1642 and 1651 and the Glorious Revolution in 1688, other events have also been crucial for the construction of the English and American "libertarian" worldview. These include the bloody civil war, waged from 1135 until 1153, between Empress Matilda (1102–1167) and usurper Stephen de Blois (1096–1154), and the so-called War of the Roses, from 1455 to 1485, between the dynasties of Lancaster and York, which was

---

11. The reign of monarch John I was discussed by David Hume in: Hume, *The History of England*, vol. 1, 407-454. Among the countless discussions regarding the legal foundations of English liberties, we recommend: Henry Maine, *Ancient Law, Its Connection with the Early History of Society, and Its Relation to Modern Ideas* (John Murray, 1861). The Humean analysis of the political and legal aspects of Anglo-Norman governments is the topic of the second appendix in Hume, *The History of England*, vol. 1, 407-454. The Kirkian perspectives on "The Reign of Law" and on "The Frame of the English Constitution" can be found in: Kirk, *The Roots of American Order*, 183-200.

brought to an end by the victory of Welsh Henry VII (1457–1509) of the House of Tudor, who implemented monarchic absolutism.[12]

Probably even more important than the various English political disputes, the matter of religious dissenters has played a major role in the constitution of the American nation. A great number of English, as well as Scottish and Irish, decided to leave the British islands and migrate to the thirteen colonies in North America, many striving to attain religious freedom, which was a demand more relevant than the pursuit of wealth for them. As will be more thoroughly discussed in the next chapter, the experience of those religious dissidents as colonists in the New World was the actual revolution from which the United States arose— that is, their resistance to the abuses of King George III (1738–1829) and the British Parliament, which led to their independence in 1776, the culmination of a long historical process.

While the independence of the United States was an act of American colonists in defense of their fundamental liberties,

---

12. See Hume, *The History of England*, vols. 1-4 for a general comprehension the English monarchy, since its early days until the end of the reign of Elizabeth I (1533-1603), the last sovereign of the Dynasty of Tudor, whereas the fifth and sixth volumes narrate the governments of the Stuart Dynasty since the ascension of James I (1566-1625) to the throne until the Glorious Revolution, in 1688.

which were threatened by impositions made by the British Crown, the protagonist of the Brazilian secession from Portuguese rule was the heir of the monarch himself, who in 1822, against the wishes of both the insurgents in Porto and the court in Lisbon, defended the autonomy of the Brazilian people. Portuguese society's elevated level of dependence on its government, a trait Brazilians have inherited from Portugal, is due to the fact that, on several occasions throughout history, the Lusitanian monarchs have effectively taken on the role of liberators of the nation against various domestic and foreign threats.

As previously stressed in this chapter, the very creation of the Kingdom of Portugal in 1139 resulted from the actions of Dom Afonso Henriques, then sovereign of the County of Portugal and later the first Portuguese monarch, who liberated his country both from the Kingdom of León and from the Muslim invaders. Unlike the British situation, the Lusitanian monarchs acted as true liberators at various times in history. This reality, on the downside, has been one of the bases for the damaging patrimonialism which to this day plagues the Brazilian motherland.

An important narrative on the constitution of the Portuguese monarchy was presented by Portuguese historian, journalist, poet, novelist, playwright, and liberal activist Alexandre Herculano (1810–1877). His *História de Portugal*, a monumental work released for the first time in four volumes published respectively in 1846, 1847, 1849, and 1853, was a pioneering effort within the Portuguese environment in regard to the adoption of a historiographic method based on the scientific method. Within that deep historical analysis, the renowned liberal thinker narrated events that had taken place from the kingdom's origins to the year 1279, discussing, in addition to the process of the creation of the Kingdom of Portugal by its first monarch, the kingdoms of his successors: Sancho I (1154–1211), Afonso II (1185–1223), Sancho II (1209–1248), and Afonso III (1210–1279).

According to Herculano, upon facing the Muslim invaders and, at the same time, achieving autonomy from the Hispanic kingdom of León, the Lusitanian monarchy was "constituted as a political individual through the efforts and tenacity of our first princes and their knights," so that, during that process, "the kingdom of Portugal was formed by the two means of revolution and conquest."[13] Furthermore, the historian stressed that, "if we are to believe old chroniclers and modern historians, the Battle of Ourique was the cornerstone of Portuguese monarchy," since, as a consequence of "such an astonishing victory," on July 25, 1139, the soldiers, the very next day, "proclaimed as king the young prince who had led them to triumph."[14]

Respecting the historical experience of the Brazilian monarch, the situation wasn't that much different than the Lusitanian tradition. As will be explained in subsequent chapters, the process

---

13. Alexandre Herculano, *Historia de Portugal desde o começo da Monarchia até o fim do reinado de Affonso III*, 8th ed., vol. 1 (Livrarias Aillaud & Bertrand, 1875), 99.

14. Herculano, *Historia de Portugal*, vol. 2, 174.

of Brazil's independence is directly linked to the transference of the Portuguese court in 1808 from Lisbon to Rio de Janeiro, with the support of the English, by King João VI (1767–1826), within the context of the invasion of the Iberian Peninsula by Napoleonic troops. The man responsible for the secession of the Brazilian nation from the United Kingdom of Portugal, Brazil, and Algarve, established in 1815, was the very heir of the Portuguese monarch, who, after having declared the independence of the new country with the "Cry of Ipiranga" on September 7, 1822, was hailed by the people as the "Constitutional Emperor and Perpetual Defender of Brazil" on October 12 of the same year. He was thereafter crowned, on December 1, 1822, and given the title of Emperor Pedro I (1798–1834). The prince-soldier liberator also reigned in Portugal over the course of two months from March to May 1826, under the title King Pedro IV, and he fathered both Portuguese queen Maria II (1819–1853) and Brazilian emperor Pedro II (1825–1891).

In the words of Brazilian historian and anthropologist Sérgio Buarque de Holanda (1902–1982), "the founders of the Brazilian Empire strayed far, save few exceptions, from wanting to make a tabula rasa of all the institutions inherited by the metropole."[15] In his 1957 treatise *A Democracia Coroada* (The Crowned Democracy), after having pointing out that "it is not possible to study

---

15. Sérgio Buarque de Holanda, *História Geral da Civilização Brasileira*, 3rd ed., tome 2, vol. 1 (DIFEL, 1970), 32.

Brazilian history without first analyzing our Portuguese predecessors," Brazilian conservative historian and Catholic philosopher João Camilo de Oliveira Torres (1915–1973) asserted that "continuity remarkably widens with the permanence of the dynasty." He stressed, moreover, that the rupture between the colony and the metropole occurred during the process of independence "in virtue of the slow-paced, safe, and smooth evolution plotted by Dom João VI," and finally concluded that "we must look for the explanation for the Cry of Ipiranga within a history begun in the Battle of Ourique."[16]

In the English experience, the opposition of the barons and clergy to the abuses of the Crown was the basis for what we now call a "civil society," as well as for the process of independence for the United States, whose actors were the American colonists, resisting the abuses committed by the British parliament and the king. Thus, in both cases, what actually occurred were movements from the bottom to the top. In contrast, within the Portuguese and Brazilian environments, from the Battle of Ourique in 1139 until the Cry of Ipiranga in 1822, the monarchs were the protagonists in the fight for freedom and justice, in a movement from the top to the bottom. In the case of Brazilian emancipation, we see a liberal-conservative action taken by Pedro I, with his regenerative project, against the revolutionary liberal members of the Courts of

---

16. João Camilo de Oliveira Torres, *A Democracia Coroada: Teoria Política do Império do Brasil* (Edições Câmara, 2017), 41.

Lisbon, who wished to reverse the condition of a united kingdom of Brazil and once more turn the territory into a colonial state.

The comments made by Portuguese historian, social scientist, and liberal parliamentarian Joaquim Pedro de Oliveira Martins (1845–1894) in his *História de Portugal* from 1879, allows a better comprehension of the first Brazilian emperor. Pedro I's mentality was forged in the profound traditions of the Lusitanian monarchy, amalgamated with the classical liberal ideas of that time, and both of these guided his actions of resistance to the determinations made by Lisbon's liberal courts in the disputes with their political opponents in Brazil and his fight against the intent of his brother Dom Miguel (1801–1866) and his absolutist partisans, who sought to usurp the throne of his daughter (the legitimate queen).

Having described Portuguese society as a "passive element" that is obedient to its governors' "whims and characters," Oliveira Martins stated that, "throughout the first three centuries, that is, during the first epoch of Portuguese history, independence is a fact emerging from the personal merit of military chiefs," and contended that, in the absence of the ideal of nationality, "regarding the personal merit of the first Portuguese monarchs, the circumstance of them being the interpreters of such a feeling should be added to it."[17] In depicting Afonso Henriques's character, the historian employed sentences that would also be suitable to por-

---

17. Joaquim Pedro de Oliveira Martins, *Historia de Portugal*, 3rd ed., vol. 1 (Livraria Bertrand, 1882), 55.

tray Pedro I, saying that "the young prince gathered all the required conditions to consolidate an independence that been hitherto precarious"; much like the first Brazilian emperor, his descendant, the first Portuguese king "was bold, reckless even, personally brave, a quality that was not all that common at the time, howbeit it might seem so to many." In the attempt to assure independence, "neither knighthood pride, nor family feelings, nor personal hatreds, nor stupendous vendettas" took over his mind, which was not occupied by "any chimera, great ambition, or poetic feeling." Oliveira Martins concluded that "the absolute predominance of a practical idea, served by a lucid intelligence, by a character devoid of greatness, and by a proven valor made him invincible, even when he was beaten."[18]

The process of independence promoted by Afonso I was but an initial stage in the consolidation of the Kingdom of Portugal, whose "idea of nation" was constituted by wars, with "sieges and campaigns" being a "regular feature"[19] during the reigns of the aforementioned Sancho I, Afonso II, Sancho II, and Afonso III. These military conflicts served to outline the frontiers of the Lusitanian monarchy against the threats posed by Muslims and neighboring Hispanic Christian monarchies. The 1249 incorporation of the region of Moorish Algarve into the Portugues Christian kingdom during the reign of Afonso III defined the country's

---

18. Oliveira Martins, *Historia de Portugal*, 66-68.

19. Oliveira Martins, *Historia de Portugal*, 83.

territory. Thus, to his son, Denis I, as well as to his successors—not only from the House of Burgundy but also from the subsequent Portuguese dynasties, "it was conceded that they should rule over the fully constituted kingdom, within the limits of its current frontiers."[20]

Kings Afonso IV (1291–1357), Pedro I (1320–1367), and Fernando I (1345–1383) were the last three members of the House of Burgundy to rule the country. Not to be confused with Brazilian emperor Pedro I— known in Portugal as Pedro IV—Portuguese king Pedro I, according to Oliveira Martins's narrative, was the true "patriarch of the Portuguese family," since his "righteous fury is not any more bizarre than the warrior-like fury of the first king," Afonso Henriques. The author added of Pedro I that "punishing the wicked, keeping the strong in check, 'wishing to provide amusement and mercy to our people,' such was his constant paternal care."[21] Nonetheless, his legitimate heir did not follow up on his political work, the reign of Fernando I being marked by much instability, which after his death brought about the first Portuguese dynastic crisis.

Thenceforth, it was up to Fernando I's half-brother, then Master Avis, who was Pedro I's bastard son, to initiate the glorious House of Aviz, under the title of King João I, whose election by the courts on April 6, 1385, was regarded as a proof "of the

---

20. Oliveira Martins, *Historia de Portugal*, 100.

21. Oliveira Martins, *Historia de Portugal*, 102-104.

nation's vitality, of its already finalized independence." However, "an acclamation" did not suffice: "a baptism was necessary for the monarchy," whose Battle of Aljubarrota on August 14, 1385, rebuffing the Castilian army, with the support of English allies, "responded to the eloquence of the courts with weapons." This military campaign is deemed the milestone that established the end of the Portuguese Middle Ages and the beginning of the modern era, as it wrapped up "the first epoch of the nation," which, again in the words of Oliveira Martins, represented the "period of its laborious and slow-paced constitution."[22]

The diplomatic, military, and commercial alliances between the British and the Portuguese which had been forged in the Middle Age by the House of Burgundy were thence reaffirmed and broadened in modernity with the ascension of the House of Aviz to the throne. The marriage between English princess Philippa of Lancaster and Portuguese king João I, produced—among their numerous offspring—not only the future king Duarte I but also the famous navigator prince Henrique, Duke of Viseu, who, according to Oliveira Martins, "was the harsh, pertinacious hero to whom Portugal owed the acknowledgement and vassalage of the entire globe."[23]

With the support of his father, João I, as well as, afterward, by his brother Duarte I, Prince Henrique issued, through the famous

---

22. Oliveira Martins, *Historia de Portugal*, 156-159.

23. Oliveira Martins, *Historia de Portugal*, 164.

School of Sagres, the necessary conditions for the enterprise of the great Portuguese navigations. This endeavor was carried out with greater intensity in the reigns of Afonso V (1432–1481), João II (1455–1495), Manuel I (1469–1521), and João III (1502–1557), and the discovery of Brazil occurred within this context. In the words of Oliveira Martins's account, "having been drawn into a maelstrom, Portugal had discovered the Atlantic islands and reached India," which gave way for a new venture to be sought, that of "devouring the discovered, digesting the world."[24]

Given the material presented in this chapter, it becomes clear that some of the heterogeneous characteristics between the United States and Brazil are rooted in the distinct ways by which a significant portion of the gentry, clergy, and other members of English and Portuguese societies engaged with their respective monarchs. Still, the relationships between government and society should not be regarded as the sole cause of the current differences between the two nations. It is also important to point out the large contrasts concerning settlement, weather, religion, economic output, and political organization, which will be the next chapter's topic.

---

24. Oliveira Martins, *Historia de Portugal*, 218.

2

PORTUGUESE AMERICA AND THE ENGLISH COLONIES

The recent rise of groups associated with the so-called "New Right," manifested in opposition to Brazil's *Partido dos Trabalhadores* (Labor Party) between 2015 and 2016, is a noteworthy development. Influenced by the United States' context, these groups adopted the label "conservative" so as to distinguish themselves from both their socialist opponents and their libertarian ("liberal") allies. This raises the question of what people believe needs to be conserved in Brazilian society. Obviously, it's hard to conserve something within an institutional environment marked by legal instability, executive and judicial authoritarianism, state interventionism, patrimonialism, generalized corruption, and revolutionary and progressive mentalities. Even though it is seemingly unclear to some of the "conservatives" grouped around the slogan "God, country, family," the most valuable patrimony to be conserved in Brazil encompasses the positive aspects inherited by the Portugues-tropical culture, such as its moral Christian basis, national unity, and several cultural elements. In this vein, according to philosopher and historian Antonio Paim (1927–2021), "in regard to the cultural dimension of colonization, the Portuguese managed to achieve a substantial unity, starting with the language."[1]

However, as is easily observed, there are within Brazilian society contradictory feelings regarding the Portuguese heritage. On one hand, there's the naïvely optimistic belief of the vainglorious, according to which Brazil is the "nation of the future," in such a way that progress will be miraculously attained in some coming time, even without citizens' virtuous and laborious efforts or the implementation of institutional reforms to assure the effectiveness of the rule of law and the free-market economy. On the other hand, many believe in the pessimistic fallacy that Brazil is doomed to economic failure and systematic corruption due to not having followed the same path toward success taken by the United States, having in mind Portuguese rather than English colonization and the Catholic religious heritage instead of a Protestant cultural basis.

In truth, the rhetoric and posture adopted by both optimistic nationalists and proponents of the "mongrel complex"—an ex-

---

1. Antonio Paim, *Momentos Decisivos da História do Brasil*, 2nd ed. (VIDE Editorial, 2014), 52.

pression coined by writer Nelson Rodrigues (1912–1980)—have justified individuals' lethargy and, consequently, state interventionism. The myth is often repeated that, throughout the first centuries of Brazil as a Portuguese colony and an independent nation, there wouldn't have been a Brazilian people but for the state, and this is used as a justification for passive acceptance of governmental intervention in society, an intervention that is regarded as the only means to reach the coveted progress.

A comparison between the distinct colonial processes of Portuguese America and the British colonies in North American may provide a better understanding of the Brazilian problem. Having discussed the colonization models adopted by the British in North America and by the Spanish in a large part of the American continent, Nobel-laureate economist Douglass North (1920–2015) stated the following:

> The contrast between the histories of England and of Spain and their colonies over the past five centuries is a sobering tale of the persistence of a path-dependent pattern of evolution. In the case of England, the Magna Carta, the evolution of secure property rights, and the eventual triumph of Parliament in 1689 were institutional stepping stones that produced political democracy and long-run economic growth—a pattern reproduced and expanded in English North America. In the case of Spain, a large, centralized bureaucracy administered an ever-growing body of de-

crees and juridical directives that defined the course of action. Every detail of the economy and polity was structured, with the objective of furthering the interests of the Crown in the creation of the most powerful empire since Rome. The ultimate consequences were repeated bankruptcies, decline, and centuries of stagnation. In the Spanish New World the pattern of centralized bureaucracies with detailed control of the polity and economy has produced three centuries of sporadic and uneven development and political instability.[2]

Nonetheless, there are significant differences in the relations between government and society in the Spanish Empire and in the Kingdom of Portugal, as well as in the colonization models employed by the two nations—especially before the Iberian Union (1580–1640), which led, in the Brazilian environment, to expressive changes. In addition to extensive state intervention in the economy, modern absolutist practices, which weren't part of the Lusitanian monarchic tradition, were implemented in the country by Fernando Álvarez de Toledo y Pimentel (1507–1582), Duke of Alba, commander of the military forces which defeated the

---

2. Douglass C. North, *Transaction Costs, Institutions, and Economic Performance* (International Center for Economic Growth, 1992), 20-21.

Portuguese troops that were loyal to Dom António (1531–1595), Prior of Crato, in the Battle of Alcântara, on August 25, 1580, during the succession crisis. In criticizing, in 1851, the absolutism of Dom Miguel's partisans, Alexandre Herculano noted that "in Portugal despotism is modern, whereas freedom is ancient."[3] In the words of João Camilo de Oliveira Torres, "Absolutism in Portugal was typically an imported good."[4]

The beginning of Brazilian history was the arrival on April 22, 1500, in what is now the city of Porto Seguro in the state of Bahia, of a fleet of caravels of the expedition bound for Calcutta, India, commanded by Pedro Álvares Cabral (1468–1520), who claimed for the Portuguese monarch the newly found land. The historiographic debate concerning the intentionality of the route deviation of the vessels westward, thence straying far from the African coasts, lingers on today. Still, the official version provided by the Portuguese court at the time was that the whole incident was but a mishap—such an explanation now regarded as an evasion to prevent any diplomatic incidents involving the Hispanic Crown. Historical sources indicate that, before the arrival of the Portuguese, Spanish navigator Vicente Yáñez Pinzón (1462–1514) had explored, in January 1500, other locales that currently belong

---

3. Alexandre Herculano, "O Paiz e a Nação" (1851), in *Opusculos*, vol. 7 (Tavares Cardoso & Irmãos, 1898), 120.

4. João Camilo de Oliveira Torres, *A Democracia Coroada: Teoria Política do Império do Brasil* (Edições Câmara, 2017), 44.

in the Brazilian territory. However, the official discovery of the country must be considered as dating from the juridical act which claimed its lands, according to the terms established by the Treaty of Tordesillas regarding the Kingdom of Portugal, which set off Brazil's colonization as part of the Portuguese maritime empire.[5]

At first, the territory was given the name of *Ilha de Vera Cruz* (Island of the True Cross) by its discoverer, whereas, later in the 1500s, this name was changed to *Terra de Santa Cruz* (Land of the Holy Cross) and, in 1534, Crown documents started referring to it as *Capitanias do Brasil* (Captaincies of Brazil). Even before the official adoption of the name by the Portuguese Crown, between 1502 and 1512—during the period when a Portuguese merchant of Jewish ancestry, Fernão de Loronha (1470–1540), whose name's corruption resulted in Fernando de Noronha, occupied the position of the territory's *Capitão Donatário* (endowed captain)—the lands on the Atlantic coast of South America that were under the authority of the Kingdom of Portugal were being called Brazil.

There is no historiographic consensus on the origin of this name. The most common explanation is that it derives from the tree called *pau-brazil* (brazilwood), the species *Paubrasilia echinata*, whose popular moniker stems from the terms *pau* (wood)

---

5. On the Portuguese maritime expansion, between the 15th and 19th centuries see C. R. Boxer *The Portuguese Seaborne Empire, 1415-1825* (Hutchinson, 1969).

and *brasa* (ember). Nonetheless, some researchers prefer the explanation that Brazil comes from the association made by Fernão de Loronha himself with the island Hy-Brasil from Irish mythology. Among the noteworthy authors who have supported this hypothesis are the English historian and poet Robert Southey (1774–1843); Brazilian historians Capistrano de Abreu (1853–1927) and Pedro Calmon (1902–1985) in their groundbreaking work; and several others who opted for a broader cultural outlook in lieu of the reductionist materialistic analysis. An important scholar who supports this view for etymological reasons is Sérgio Buarque de Holanda, who affirmed in his classic 1959 study *Visões do Paraíso* (Views on Paradise) that the country's name "appears more to be the toponym of the Irish *Hy Bressail* and *O'Brazil*, which supposedly mean 'fortunate island.' That reason, more plausible than others, could explain the alternative names of 'O brasil' and 'Obrasil' featured in several maps."[6]

Grounded in both the archetypical outlook provided by the psychology of Carl Jung (1875–1961) and in the classical or conservative conceptions of Locke, Burke, Tocqueville, and Hayek, and in dialogue with several Brazilian historiographic discussions, diplomat and political scientist José Osvaldo de Meira Penna

---

6. Sérgio Buarque de Holanda, *Visão do Paraíso: Os motivos edênicos no descobrimento e colonização do Brasil*, 2nd ed. (Brasiliense/Publifolha, 2000), 209.

(1917–2017), after having mapped the national psychology,[7] not only backed up the theory of the origins of the country's name in the Irish myth of Hy-Brasil island but also demonstrated that, in various aspects, such a medieval utopia molded, within the Brazilian collective unconscious, an idyllic outlook, according to which, with Brazil being a land of abundance and great riches, it might be possible to achieve prosperity without the need for hard labor.[8] As depicted in several medieval maps, the utopian locality within the Atlantic would be one of the fortunate islands discovered by the legendary naval expedition led by monk Brendan of Clonfert (484–577), the Navigator, a place filled with riches.[9] Out of curiosity, it is worth pointing out that, in his essay "On Fayre Stories," in discussing the problem of the excessive rationalization of knowledge in modernity, philologist and literary scholar J. R. R. Tolkien (1892–1973) claimed:

---

7. José Osvaldo de Meira Penna, *Psicologia do Subdesenvolvimento*, 2nd ed. (VIDE Editorial, 2017).

9. The narrative of the trip appears in the Latin work *Navigatio Sancti Brendani Abbatis* [Voyage of Saint Brendan the Abbot], written around the year of 900. For an analysis of the myth of Hy-Brazil, see Barbara Freitag, *Hy Brasil: The Metamorphosis of an Island, from cartographic error to Celtic Elysium* (Rodopi, 2013).

> It seems to become fashionable soon after the great voyages had begun to make the world seem too narrow to hold both men and elves; when the magic land of *Hy Breasail* in the West had become the mere Brazils, the land of red-dye-wood.[10]

Along with the rationalist and materialistic conceptions, the fact that brazilwood smugglers were nicknamed "Brazilians" was one of the factors that led a substantial portion of historians to be receptive to the theory that the name of the country is associated with the Southern American coast's native tree. However, teaching only that version induces a consolidation within the Brazilian mind of a simplistic perception of the motherland's history, which, considering the use of Marxist categories by nearly all teachers and most textbooks, reinforces three fallacious myths about Brazil.

The first fallacy is the idea that Brazilian colonization, similarly to what occurred in Spanish America, was motivated purely by the wish to exploit natural resources. Such an economistic view, based on Marxist theories, neglects the fact that Portugal's endeavor also exhibited two religious aspects. On one hand, the main intent of many Portuguese colonizers was the evangelization of the New World, as is highlighted by the actions of Jesuit missionaries, es-

---

10. J. R. R. Tolkien, "On Fairy-Stories", in *The Monsters and the Critics and Othes Essays*, ed. Christopher Tolkien (George Allen and Unwin, 1983), 111.

pecially Father José de Anchieta, SJ (1534–1597), the Apostle of Brazil,[11] and the members of the *Ordem de Cristo* (Military Order of Christ), who collaborated actively with the grand Portuguese navigations, alongside other religious military orders.[12] On the other hand, the "fortunate lands" in South America drew in many "New Christians," Jews who had been forced into conversion and who settled in Brazil to escape possible persecution by the Inquisition and to attempt to create a land of freedom and prosperity.[13]

The second misconception with respect to Brazil's colonial origins is the simplistic idea, inspired by Marxist theses, which describes the Brazilian economic history as a succession of five stages. According to this schematic perspective, Brazil's development proceeded in stages, each dominated by a distinct monoculture. Throughout the first half of the sixteenth century, there was

---

11. Helen G. Dominian, *Apostle of Brazil: The Biography of Padre José de Anchieta, S.J. (1534–1597)* (Exposition Press, 1958).

12. Fernanda Olival, *The Military Orders and the Portuguese Expansion (15th to 17th Centuries)* (Baywolf Press/The Portuguese Studies Review, 2018).

13. Geraldo Pieroni, "Outcasts from the Kingdom: The Inquisition and the Banishment of New Christians to Brazil," in *The Jews and the Expansion of Europe to the West, 1450-1800*, eds. Paolo Bernardini and Norman Fiering (Berghahn Books, 2001), 242-54.

the so-called "brazilwood cycle." Between the second half of the sixteenth century and the mid-eighteenth century, the "sugarcane cycle" prevailed. The second half of the eighteenth century, the theory continues, was the "gold cycle." From the mid-nineteenth century, during the empire, up until the first three decades of the twentieth century, the period of the Old Republic, the "coffee cycle" predominated. Finally, from the 1930s on, during the Vargas era, the "industrialization cycle" emerged, marked by "national-developmentalism." The division of Brazilian economic history into those five periods tends to either neglect or minimize the diversity of productive activities carried out in distinct regions of the continental Brazilian territory over the course of the five stages, and the fact that the predominance of the exportation of one good during a given cycle does not mean the extinction of the previous cycle.

Even before his well-known 1944 debate with Eugênio Gudin over the role of the state within the nation's industrial development (see introduction), Roberto Simonsen laid the foundations of the widely disseminated theory of Brazilian economic history as divided into five stages. Simonsen did not turn to Marxism's theoretical apparatus but instead admired the interventionist state capitalism model implemented by the New Deal in the United States. In a series of writings beginning in the late 1930s, he laid the groundwork for the five-stage theory: a 1937 analysis of the Brazilian colonial economy between 1500 and 1820 in his monumental

História Econômica do Brasil (Economic History of Brazil);[14] a 1939 report on the national industrialization process, "Evolução Industrial do Brasil" (Industrial Evolution of Brazil)[15] —a study done for the *Conselho Federal de Comércio Exterior* (Federal Foreign Trade Council) during the occasion of a visit of American students to the country; and a treatment of the development of Brazilian coffee-grower culture in his 1940 essay "Aspectos da História Econômica do Café" (Aspects of the Economic History of Coffee).[16] In conceiving a historical foundation for his developmental theses, Simonsen outlined an innovative path that was then followed by two prominent Marxist Brazilian authors who added Marxist conceptions and new empirical data to Simonsen's perspective. Historian and geographer Caio Prado Júnior (1907–1990), in his 1942 book *Formação do Brasil Contemporâ-*

---

14. Roberto Simonsen, *História Econômica do Brasil: 1500-1820*, 4th ed. (Senado Federal, 2005).

15. Roberto Simonsen, "Evolução Industrial do Brasil," in Roberto Simonsen, *Evolução Industrial do Brasil e outros estudos* (Editora Nacional/Editora da USP, 1973), 5-55.

16. Roberto Simonsen, "Aspectos da História Econômica do Café," in Simonsen, *Evolução Industrial do Brasil e outros estudos*, 163-234.

neo (Formation of Contemporary Brazil)[17] and economist Celso Furtado (1920–2004), in his 1959 *Formação Econômica do Brasil* (Economic formation of Brazil),[18] solidified the current outlook on Brazilian economic history.

There are not broad and systematic works that address the history of Brazilian economic development from a perspective different from the hegemonic view mentioned above. Nevertheless, empirical data and major studies on particular topics or specific moments in Brazilian economic history, especially during the colonial and imperial periods, refute the prevailing explanation presented in the works of Simonsen, Prado Júnior, Furtado, and the other scholars who align with them— among whom are most American Brazilianists.

A brief statement of some facts on the Brazilian economy during the empire shall demonstrate the reductionist character of the economic-cycles thesis. During the term of the "coffee cycle," aside from the domestic market's varied agricultural production and the emergence of industrial activities, the country was a great exporter of several other products. In 1820 French painter Jean-Baptiste Debret (1763–1848) designed a flag model for the Royal Prince of the United Kingdom of Portugal, Brazil and Algarves, the fu-

---

17. Caio Prado Júnior, *The Colonial Background of Modern Brazil* (University of California Press, 1967).

18. Celso Furtado, *The Economic Growth of Brazil: A Survey from Colonial to Modern Times* (Praeger, 1984).

ture first emperor of Brazil. The artist created a green rectangular pavilion—the color of the House of Bragança—and placed inside it a yellow diamond—the color of the House of Habsburg. Within the diamond—aside from the Cross of the Order of Christ, an armillary sphere, and a crown and stars, symbolizing the provinces within the Kingdom of Brazil— there were representations of a flowering tobacco branch and a sugarcane stem. When this version was adapted in 1822 to be used as the flag of the Empire of Brazil, among other tiny alterations, the sugarcane was replaced by coffee. This symbolism not only highlighted the way coffee agriculture was emerging but also showed the continued importance of the sugar sector—still true today—and of tobacco production, among other agricultural products. Even though coffee was predominant among exported products throughout the twentieth century, Brazil was also a relevant part of the international market in sugar, rubber, cotton, leather, and other agricultural derivatives, tobacco, yerba-maté, wood, and various minerals.

The third fallacious belief regarding colonial Brazil is that the creation of the state preceded the emergence of Brazilian society. That sort of understanding tends to neglect or diminish the crucial work of evangelization performed by Christian missionaries, especially Jesuits, whose work was responsible for the formation of settlements in various areas within the territory of Portuguese America, such villages being the origin of most of Brazil's great cities.

Even before Portuguese king João III established in 1534 the colonial model which, like the medieval fiefdoms, divided Brazilian territory into fourteen hereditary captaincies that were bestowed on twelve recipients, the king ordered the 1530–1532 expedition to explore the Brazilian shoreline led by Portuguese nobleman Martim Afonso de Sousa (1500–1564). Explorers settled in Gohayó Island, located in the current state of São Paulo, and founded on January 22, 1532, São Vicente Village, whose founder ordered the construction of a church, houses, administrative buildings, a pillory, and fortifications. That first urban settlement in the nation kept evolving until it became the current capital of São Vicente, one of the fifteen seaside resorts in São Paulo.

It is worth noting that, as occurred in all of the Kingdom of Portugal's municipalities, and later, in the Empire of Brazil, that pioneering village of Portuguese America witnessed the first democratic experience in all the Americas, nearly a century prior to the pioneers who docked in 1620 in New England. On August 22, 1532, the first election for the representatives to city hall took place. Yet, despite the countless villages that were created between the sixteenth and eighteenth centuries in different regions within Portuguese America—all of them with the democratic participation of free men—the emergence of Brazilian society should not be seen as mirroring the European urban experiences or the settlements created by the Pilgrims in North America. The colonization led by the Portuguese was closer to the English experiment in the southern United States. Though the latter saw less urbanization than Brazil, the plantations in both the Old South and Brazil were constituted as dynamic farming communities.

In the period between the last decades of the sixteenth century and the mid-seventeenth century, there flourished along the Brazilian shoreline, especially in the northeastern region of the South American territory, a notable agrarian civilization managed by the private sector, which, in several aspects, may be compared to the current agricultural business model in Brazil, combining technological innovations with hard labor. While bureaucratic authorities of the Portuguese colonial state exerted control over small seaside areas, the exploitation of a larger part of the coast and of most of Portuguese America's countryside—as well as of lands belonging to the Spanish Crown, later incorporated into Brazil—was undertaken by plantation owners, Jesuit missionaries, and *bandeirantes*.

In his study outlining the most important aspects in the history of Brazil, after discussing historiographic questions and pointing out the elements that made up Brazilian culture, Antonio Paim presented a narrative divided into three decisive moments. Regarding the first stage, the colonial period, Paim concluded that Brazil, though richer than the United States, opted for poverty. Concerning the second stage, the monarchic experience of the independent nation, he pointed out how Brazil kept its national unity and left the consolidation of the representative system unfinished. Addressing the third moment, the Republican period, which is ongoing, Paim discussed how Brazil came to be structured as a unitarian national state in its patrimonial form, completed the industrial revolution, and accepted the inability to organize its political representation.

In his analysis of the first stage, after describing both the organization of productive activities and the territorial occupation throughout the first centuries and the importance of the sugar enterprise, Paim discussed how the Inquisition was responsible for imposing in Brazil the option for poverty. Backed by vast documentation and historiographic analyses, the author demonstrated that, at the time of the Spanish rule over the House of Habsburg, under the reign of King João V (1689–1750), as several persecutions of the entrepreneurs responsible for sugar production (most of them New Christians) were set in motion, the fundamental bases of Brazilian wealth were destroyed and, moreover, Counter-Reformation values opposed to profit were spread, which resulted in the discouragement of a work ethic. After elaborating on some characteristics of the formation of the United States during the seventeenth century, Paim presented a comparison between American and Brazilian trajectories over the course of the eighteenth century, concluding thus:

> By the end of that last century, Brazil and the United States had a similar number of inhabitants, which hovered around three million people. The radical distinction consisted of the moral basis and cultural traditions that were thriving. Among Americans, there was the predominance of the (Puritan) conviction that success in labor (and, therefore, enrichment) could be a sign of salvation. Among Brazilians,

who had the identical purpose of saving one's soul, there was the frank choice of poverty.[19]

This excerpt stresses the fundamental distinction between colonists in New England and *bandeirantes* in Brazil. In his notable book, mentioned earlier, Clodomir Vianna Moog, besides discussing the differences between the conquest of Brazil by the *bandeirantes* and the colonization of the United States by the pioneers, also assessed the discrepancies between the two groups, encompassing racial and geographic aspects as well as ethical and economic beliefs. This work traced the endurance of certain symbols in both cultures and pointed out the problems faced by the two nations in the contemporary process of the "massification" of society.

According to Vianna Moog, the culture of the United States "largely resulted from the efforts made by pioneers," whereas Brazil "is, to the same extent, the work of *bandeirantes*."[20] After rejecting racial determinism and highlighting the importance of geographic distinctions, the text discussed the errors inherent to economistic conceptions, such as the Marxist one, and emphasized the need for a comprehension grounded in ethical-religious differences, which better serve to explain the divergent experiences.

---

19. Paim, *Momentos Decisivos da História do Brasil*, 175.

20. Clodomir Viana Moog, *Bandeirantes e Pioneiros: Paralelo entre duas culturas* (Editora Globo, 1957), 9-10.

Vianna Moog stressed that in the composition of North American culture there was "a meaning that was initially spiritual, organic, and constructive," whereas the predominant mindset in Brazil was "predatory, extractive, and only secondarily religious."[21]

Unlike the Spanish conquests on the American continent, English colonization in North American did not derive from the statist eagerness to build an empire. Similar to what occurred in Portuguese America before the Iberian union, the British Crown offered colonial titles to different sorts of individuals, who can be divided into merchants, religious idealists, and adventurous aristocrats. Throughout the colonial period and later moments in American history, such as the gold rush in the Old West, the adventurous ones, who sought to attain great riches without much effort, bear resemblance to the figure of Brazilian *bandeirantes*, who scoured the territory in search of silver, gold, and gems. Yet the main protagonists of English colonization in North American were the merchants and rural producers in the North and South, the religious idealists who are analogous with the plantation masters and Jesuits in Brazil.

The first English attempt at colonization in North America was the adventure financed by Sir Walter Raleigh (1552–1618), who, bearing a royal charter conferred by Elizabeth I (1533–1603), invested in the establishment of the colony called Virginia (an homage to the virgin queen), in Roanoke Island, located in the

---

21. Moog, *Bandeirantes e Pioneiros*, 129.

current state of North Carolina. After two failed attempts, from 1585 to 1586 and from 1587 to 1590, the project was abandoned. In 1606, a royal charter from James I (1566–1625) to the Virginia Company authorized commercial planting in North American, whereby, in 1607, nearly a hundred men disembarked in Chesapeake Bay, initiating American colonization. For over a century, Jamestown was the only actual city in the entire region. The efforts of John Smith (1580–1631) prevented the colony from meeting the same as Roanoke Island, and John Rolfe (1585–1622) reinforced the potential of cultivating tobacco for export.

Between 1619 and 1622, around 3,570 British migrated to the colony. However, the mortality rate was extremely high, with an average of three deaths for every four people. In 1622, an indigenous attack killed 347 colonials, which led the survivors to consider leaving the territory. The solution was provided by the monarch, who in 1624 dissolved the Virginia Company and turned the region into a royal colony, appointing a governor and a counselor. Despite the fact that the Crown took responsibility for the colonials, the main decisions were taken by a democratic assembly, which in 1634 divided Virginia into eight counties, each of them governed by a justice of the peace. Up until the mid-nineteenth century, these municipal courts were the center of social, political, and commercial life in the area. Most colonials were dispersed throughout the territory and isolated on the tobacco plantations, which delayed the establishment of churches and schools. Similar to the Brazilian mills, Virginia's aristocratic and patriarchal pattern was adopted in other Southern colonies. According to Russell

Kirk, "the Virginian gentleman-planter is best remembered as one type of this class of leaders—in part because the 'Virginia Dynasty' of American presidents were members of that class."[22]

Notwithstanding the great importance of the Southern model, the true paradigm of American colonization was the settlement of New England, created by pilgrims, a group of religious dissidents, mostly Puritans, who sought in the New World the means to preserve their faith's identity. In 1620, the Plymouth colony was founded by William Bradford (1590–1657), the leader of the group of a little over a hundred people who, due to a navigation error while heading to Virginia aboard the *Mayflower*, disembarked on Plymouth Rock instead, where the letters patent of the Virginia Company were not valid. Such humble farmers, to prevent the rise of anarchy within the community, designed the Mayflower Compact, a pact that established certain common efforts for the formation of a civil body.

The ascension to the throne of Charles I (1600–1649) in 1625 provoked the migration to the region of more Puritans, who felt threatened by religious persecutions. In that process, it is worth highlighting the 1630 foundation, by John Winthrop (1606–1676), of Massachusetts, which by the year 1640 had welcomed around twenty thousand new inhabitants. Besides absorbing Plymouth, Massachusetts gave birth to the colonies of New

---

22. Russell Kirk, *The Roots of American Order*, 4th ed. (ISI Books, 2003), 317.

Hampshire, Connecticut, and Rhode Island, all of which were rooted in the same principles.

Unlike what occurred with the Southern agrarian model, the public life in the colonies in New England had a high rate of urban development, marked by the prosperity of trade and the naval construction. The most important city in the area was Boston, which in a short time became one of the largest harbors in America and the first great center that irradiated culture within the new society forged by the pioneers. The condensed settlements within the region allowed for the flourishing of countless schools, churches, and meetinghouses. In such urban communities, the people believed in the rigor of the law, enforced by elected magistrates, and the churches did not get involved in public issues, a spirit of religious tolerance accepting the various religious denominations . These factors created a land of freedom, opportunity, and prosperity for everyone who was willing to work for their own interests without undermining others. In his classic analysis of American society, Alexis de Tocqueville (1805–1859) explained the situation:

> The English colonies, and this was one of the principal causes of their prosperity, always enjoyed more internal liberty and more political independence than the colonies of other peoples; but nowhere

was this principle of liberty more completely applied than in the states of New England.[23]

The ideal of ordered liberty which structures United States society is not a revolutionary invention that emerged during the process of independence, but rather a practice that's inherent to the colonial experience and supported by a profound religious ethic. In his assessment, Vianna Moog describes American colonists in this way:

> The first settlers of the English colonies in America, especially the *Mayflower* Puritans, did not come into the New World merely or predominantly seeking gold and silver mines and easily attainable riches. Rather, they were beset by the persecution in their motherland, in search of lands where they could worship their God, read and interpret the Bible, work, help each other, and celebrate their faith in their own way. Having embarked, and bringing with them all their belongings, women, and children, they turned their backs on Europe in order to found, on this side of the Atlantic, a new homeland, the

---

23. Alexis de Tocqueville, *Democracy in America*, vol. 1 (Liberty Fund, 2012), 60.

Calvinists' theocratic homeland. They did not fathom the possibility of going back.

Conversely, the author stressed that many Portuguese who came to Brazil, having left their wives, children, and friends behind in Europe, "came with their eyes already dilated by greed." They were "initially, conquerors, not colonizers, just as later on they would turn out to be *bandeirantes* rather than pioneers." Despite the problems highlighted by the author, such Portuguese pathfinders weren't without merit. In the second of the six lectures that he delivered at Indiana State University in 1944, Gilberto Freyre underscored that, within the colonization of Brazil, there were two key figures: the "vertical founders," plantation owners who, in a settled manner, took deeper root in the land and, while maintaining certain feudal aristocratic habits, built a sophisticated civilization; and the "horizontal founders," represented by the *bandeirantes*, who in nomadic fashion explored the jungle and the backlands in search of riches.

Freyre portrayed this latter group as simple, even rustic people, on one hand, and, on the other, as individuals endowed with a bold independence of action, as they enjoyed more liberties—including the not-so-Christian one of having many women, not only white but also indigenous and black-skinned.[24] In his pioneering work, Robert Southey described the importance of the *bandeirantes*:

> While the Spaniards on the Paraguay remained where Yrala left them,... neglected after the discoveries which the first conquerors had made,... suffered the paths which they had opened to be overgrown,... and almost laid aside the manners and even the language of Spain, the Brazilians continued for two centuries to explore the country; months and years would these persevering adventurers continue among the woods and mountains, hunting slaves, or seeking for gold and jewels after the reports of the natives; and ultimately they succeeded in securing for themselves and for the House of Braganza the richest mines, and largest portion of South America, the finest region of the whole habitable earth.[25]

Released in three volumes (1810, 1817, and 1819), the thorough work by Robert Southey on Brazilian colonial history, which encompasses the period between 1500 and 1808, continues to

---

24. Gilberto Freyre, *Brazil: An Interpretation* (Knopf, 1945), 35-65.

25. Robert Southey, *History of Brazil – Part the First*, 2nd ed. (Longman, Hurst, Rees Orme, and Brown, 1822), 346.

be the broadest and most systematic analysis in English on the topic. As the proprietor of the largest and best collection in England of books and documents on Portugal, Spain, and their overseas possessions, Southey wrote the first Brazilian general history, wherein, from a conservative perspective, he integrated the Brazilian colonial experience with the context of modern European civilization.[26] The poet and historian Southey was deeply influenced by Edmund Burke (1729–1797); like his friends William Wordsworth (1770–1850) and Samuel Taylor Coleridge (1772–1834), he abandoned in adulthood his juvenile sympathies for Rousseaunian sentimentalism, French Revolution ideals, and the anarchic progressivism of William Godwin (1756–1836), in favor of a conservative disposition.[27] Having highlighted his intention of maintaining the link between moral and cultural values from the past and the future, Southey used the narrative of Brazilian history to develop important political and religious r

---

26. Geoffrey Carnall, *Robert Southey and His Age: The Development of a Conservative Mind* (Hassell Street Press, 2021).

27. Alfred Cobban, *Edmund Burke and the Revolt against the Eighteenth Century: A Study of the Political and Social Thinking of Burke, Wordsworth, Coleridge and Southey* (AMS Press, 1929).

28. Stuart Andrews, *Robert Southey: History, Politics and Religion* (Palgrave, 2011).

eflections.[28] His analyses represent a conservative view on how Portuguese colonizers, more than any other European peoples, were able to adapt to the tropics, revealing the endeavor's civilizational mixture, which mingled also Native Americans and African blacks, thence constituting a unique Portuguese-tropical culture.[29] Among the authors influenced by Southey's work, one might highlight the scholar responsible for the dissemination of Burkean thinking in Portuguese, José da Silva Lisboa (1656–1835), Viscount of Cairu, who employed, in the narrative he wrote on the first years of the Brazilian Empire, the trilogy of the English poet as a historiographic source and theoretical basis.[30]

Anticipating Freyrean thinking, Robert Southey discussed miscegenation as a positive phenomenon, as it constituted "a physical improvement, and a great political advantage."[31] In his classic

---

28. Stuart Andrews, *Robert Southey: History, Politics and Religion* (Palgrave, 2011).

29. Robert Arthur Humphreys, *Robert Southey and his History of Brazil* (Hispanic and Luso-Brazilian Council, 1978).

30. José da Silva Lisboa, *História dos Principais Sucessos Políticos do Império do Brazil*, 4 vols. (Typograhia Imperial e Nacional, 1826-1830).

31. Robert Southey, *History of Brazil – Part the Third* (Longman, Hurst, Rees Orme, and Brown, 1819), 707.

volume *The Masters and the Slaves*, Freyre addressed racial interaction in its multiple aspects, noting that "the advantage of miscegenation in Brazil ran parallel to the tremendous disadvantage of syphilis," for both "began operating at the same time: one to form the Brazilian, the ideal type of modem man for the tropics, a European with Negro or Indian blood to revive his energy; the other to deform him." Freyre thus responded to a common confusion, whereby many attributed to "miscegenation effects that are chiefly due to syphilis."[32]

More than a mere analysis of racial issues, the goal of Freyrean sociology, according to João Camilo de Oliveira Torres, was to "establish the history of Brazilian society, considering the family as its pillar."[33] Before concluding that the experience of miscegenation in Brazil constituted a victory of the human factor over economic interests, Freyre argued:

> The love of a man for his woman, and the love of a father for his children, lying above color, race, class, and social status prejudices, granted miscegenation in Brazil its most human and, at the same time, most

---

32. Gilberto Freyre, *The Masters and the Slaves: A Study in the Development of Brazilian Civilization*, 2nd ed. (Knopf, 1956), 70-71.

33. João Camilo de Oliveira Torres, *Interpretação da Realidade Brasileira* (Edições Câmara, 2017), 117.

Christian expression, without it having ceased to show its other side: the one of lust, voluptuousness, the one of brutal abuses committed against indigenous or African women by white men.[34]

Adopting the distinction made by T. S. Eliot (1888–1965) regarding the "theological" and "sociological" aspects of the ideal of a Christian society,[35] the Brazilian scholar saw "the amplitude of Christianity as an immense cultural park, to which Brazil belongs as a result of the effort of Portuguese colonization."[36] Grounded in this view of religion, "Gilberto Freyre established, in several of his works, that Portugal had adopted a 'Christocentric' rather than an 'ethnocentric' concept of colonization," for "racial differences disappeared in face of the unity of faith."[37] Freyre himself claimed that Infante Dom Henrique "decisively concurred so as

---

34. Gilberto Freyre, *O Mundo que o Português Criou: Aspectos das relações sociais e de cultura do Brasil com Portugal e as colônias portuguesas* (É Realizações, 2010), 27.

35. T. S. Elliot, *The Idea of a Christian Society* (Faber and Faber, 1939).

36. Gilberto Freyre, *Uma Cultura Ameaçada e Outros Ensaios* (É Realizações, 2010), 54.

37. Torres, *Interpretação da Realidade Brasileira*, 254.

to provide for the relationships between Europeans and non-Europeans, between white people and colored people, a particularly Portuguese-Christian direction," which made it possible for a necessary encounter between the East and the West to occur, and concluded, furthermore, that such a process only took place through "the miscegenation and interpenetration of cultures,"[38]

Deemed decisive for the constitution of the nation, the Battle of Guararapes amalgamated the elements of miscegenation and religion. Waged April 18–19, 1648, the battle featured Brazilian forces led by the Caucasian André Vidal de Negreiros (1606–1689), the indigenous Filipe Camarão (1600-1648), the African American Henrique Dias (d. 1662), and the mixed-race João Fernandes Vieira (1610–1681), whose goal was to expel the Flemish from Brazil. In addition to their military spirit, the Portuguese-Brazilian combatants were inspired by a religious outlook, fed by a sermon proclaimed in 1640 by Jesuit Father Antônio Vieira (1608–1697), who advocated the campaign as a sort of crusade to defend the Catholic faith from the Calvinist menace. The Dutch presence in Brazil put the Lusitanian project at risk, a fact that was acknowledged even by the Protestant Southey, who, having discussed the way such a threat had been foreseen and announced by Father

---

38. Gilberto Freyre, *O Luso e o Trópico: Sugestões em torno dos métodos portugueses de integração de povos autóctones e de culturas diferentes da europeia num complexo novo de civilização* (É Realizações, 2010), 21.

Vieira, emphasized that the site where the battle occurred was "the most memorable scene in the military history of Brazil," for, even with the prolongation of the war for a few more years, "this victory decided the fate of Brazil."[39] In a parliamentary speech delivered in 1948, Gilberto Freyre stressed that, during the military campaign, "Brazil's address" had been written "in blood: the one of not only one or two Brazils, but three," seeing that, from Guararapes, there emerged "a fraternally mestizo Brazil in race and culture, rather than another South American republic roughly nativist or aggressively anti-European, or another Java, or even a huge Guiana."[40]

Even though they were, to a higher or lesser degree, critics of profit, the Jesuits, from José de Anchieta to Antônio Vieira, constituted an important civilizational force in Brazil, trying to establish by means of religion and education the foundations for the flourishing of a genuine Christian society. Such a process was interrupted by Sebastião José de Carvalho e Melo (1699–1782), Marquis of Pombal, minister of King José I (1714–1777), when he decreed on September 3, 1759, that Jesuits should be expelled from Portugal and its colonies, thus anticipating the persecutions executed in other countries and the eventual suppression of the re-

---

39. Southey, *History of Brazil – Part the Third*, 203-204.

40. Gilberto Freyre, "Louvor a Guararapes," in Vamireh Chacon, *Discursos Parlamentares* (Câmara dos Deputados, 1994), 161.

ligious order.[41] The quarrel with the Jesuits was not the only negative consequence stemming from Pombal's reforms. According to Antonio Paim, his artificial attempts to modernize Portugal, besides failing to address "the reformation of political institutions," reinforced the mercantilist notion that international commerce "should be directly subordinate to the state or closely supervised by it."[42] The figure of the Portuguese enlightened despot preceded the Brazilian positivists of the nineteenth century, who were responsible for the diffusion of pragmatism and irrationalism typical of the "Brazilian educational philosophy," which, according to João Camilo de Oliveira Torres, "derives from Pombal and his reformation of the University of Coimbra."[43] Even anticlerical historian Joaquim Pedro de Oliveira Martins acknowledged that Pombal "assumed that, in Portugal, the collective temper was one similar to that of England or Flanders, as philosophy, absolutist and classical, did not yet acknowledge that societies grow and also

---

41. See Jean Lacouture, "Expelled Like Dogs," in *Jesuits: A Multibiography*, trans. Jeremy Leggatt (Counterpoint, 1995), 261-97 and William V. Bangert S.J., "Exile, Suppression and Restoration," in *A History of the Society of Jesus* (Institute of Jesuit Sources, 1972), 363-430.

42. Paim, *Momentos Decisivos da História do Brasil*, 187.

43. João Camilo de Oliveira Torres, *O Positivismo no Brasil* (Edições Câmara, 2018), 34-35.

live as plants, according to their seeds, the weather, the air they breathe, the waters that shower them."[44]

In explaining the persistent Brazilian delay in economic development, Antonio Paim enumerated the following reasons: (1) patrimonialism, inherited by Portugal and intensified during the Vargas era; (2) the profit-inhibitor ethics propagated from the time of the Inquisition at the end of the sixteenth century to the contemporary rise of liberation theology; (3) the scientific mentality which, instituted by Marquis of Pombal, was updated by positivism, Varguism, and Marxism.[45] The great challenge faced by Brazilian liberals and conservatives, at distinct junctures, has been the overcoming of those three factors, which are responsible for the nation's backwardness, in such a way that it is possible to make the much-desired free and prosperous society of the future flourish.

---

44. Joaquim Pedro de Oliveira Martins, *Historia de Portugal*, 3rd ed., vol. 2 (Livraria Bertrand, 1882), 190.

45. Antonio Paim, *O Relativo Atraso Brasileiro e sua Difícil Superação* (Editoria SENAC, 2000).

3

TWO LIBERAL PROCESSES OF INDEPENDENCE

In the 1760s, when new tensions emerged in North American society in response to the creation of taxes established by the British Parliament without the consent of the English colonies, the territory bound to become Brazil still constituted Portuguese America. However, the situation was not without noise and tension; the complexity of the clashing interests was already the cause of conflicts, known among Brazilians as nativist uprisings.[1]

---

1. This term *nativist* in this Brazilian context has a different meaning from that typical of American history. In the United States, nativism usually connotes anti-immigrant sentiment, while in Brazil nativist uprisings were revolts by Brazilians against Portuguese colonialism.

Over a century before the notorious episode that occurred on December 16, 1773, and became known as the "Boston Tea Party," the city of Rio de Janeiro experienced the Cachaça Revolt, also known as "Barbalho's Revolt" or "Bernarda." Between November 8, 1660, and April 6, 1661, Brazilians rebelled against the Portuguese monopoly on wine and brandy—*bagaceira*, made of the pomace of wine grapes—as well as against the taxation of such goods. The result, despite military repression of the upheaval, was that the Crown initially ceased seizing contraband and, in 1695, authorized sugarcane brandy (*cachaça*) production in Brazil. Shortly thereafter, subsequent conflicts, such as the Beckman Revolt in 1684, the Emboabas War from 1707 to 1709 in São Paulo, or the Mascate War from 1710 to 1711 in Pernambuco, manifested open objection to the pretensions of the native colonial elite and the *reinós*—that is, the Portuguese, or better yet, the Portuguese from Portugal, since it would be anachronistic to speak concretely of a Brazilian national aspiration. The magic word "republic" was already being heard during the War of the Mascates, when authorities denounced the penetration of Enlightenment ideals, effervescent in European culture, into colonial society. At the same time, obviously devoid of the influence of any Enlightenment principles, runaway slaves kept insurgent strongholds, creating their own societies, *quilombos*, among which stood out the Palmares Quilombo, which resisted the authorities of the Lusitanian Crown for eight decades.

In 1776, when the founding fathers of the United States, representing their thirteen colonies, gathered to promote separation from the United Kingdom and declare the independence of the nation, they ended up inspiring much more than the mere emergence of a future global power. The movement of 1776 represented a practical example of the possibility opened up by John Locke (1632–1704), who had suggested that individuals could rebel against injustice and tyranny through an "appeal to heaven."[2]

Simultaneously, the American process of independence was a pioneering case of a political community whose constitution had been grounded on the theories of representation and liberty entertained by Enlightenment philosophers, yet pegged to the defense of order (without implying any paradox whatsoever), and anchored in a Protestant religious tradition as well as in the thinking of British neo-republicans who preceded the Lockean system and in the classical political literature of Greeks and Romans. After all, as maintained by Russell Kirk, the cultural and institutional formation of the United States was a legacy blended from Israel, Greco-Roman civilization, medieval tradition, and modernity.[3]

In that sense—and unlike what occurred with the French revolutionaries of 1789 or the leaders of the Spanish colonies' indepen-

---

2. John Locke, *Two Treatises of Government*, in *The Works of John Locke*, vol. 5 (Thomas Tegg, W. Sharpe and Son, 1823), 179.

3. Russell Kirk, *The Roots of American Order*, 4th ed. (ISI Books, 2003).

dence movements in the early nineteenth century—the founding fathers did not adhere to the rationalist ideological project of inventing a new humanity, even though the process is known as the American "Revolution," for in fact, the event in the United States could best be defined as a kind of counter-revolution, supported both by the concrete experience of freedom which prevailed in the British and American colonial societies and the theoretical principles of a kind of moderate liberalism as well as a non-reactionary conservatism.[4]

A new generation of nativist riots would emerge by the end of the century in Portuguese America, clearly inspired by the North American phenomenon. Thus, it is noticeable that the so-called American Revolution impressed the Brazilian elite at the time, who encountered it through the work *Révolution de l'Amérique* (The Revolution of America), by Guillaume-Thomas François-Raynal (1713–1796), abbot Raynal. According to the explanation given by Antonio Paim, Raynal's writing, which can be found in several colonial libraries and was supportive of the opening of Brazilian trade to all nations, was highly sympathetic

---

4. Such counter-revolutionary perspective regarding the formation of the United States was presented more explicitly by the Kirkian thought in Russell Kirk, "A Revolution Not Made, but Prevented," in *Rights and Duties: Reflections on Our Conservative Constitution*, ed. Mitchell S. Muncy (Spence Publishing Company, 1997), 47-60.

to the revolution in the thirteen colonies, and it was a wake-up call "for the Spanish and Portuguese leadership based in America regarding freedom," as well as an inspiration for

> the hope of establishing a state that would meet their actual interests. Nonetheless, in regard to the path toward the institutionalization of a new regime, the book is not instructive. The uniqueness of the British political organization is not even mentioned. Although it denies the possibility of direct democracy in nations of great territorial extensions, it does not specifically address the representative system.[5]

Consequently, the previous experiences of the insurrections against Portugal under Illuminist influence did not achieve the construction of the representative system which, in the United States, derived above all from the community life within the very colonies that joined in rebellion, having each of them sent their deputies to the Second Continental Congress in Philadelphia. All of the Brazilian uprisings, in contrast, were ill-fated. There were, for example, the Pernambucan convulsions, where the leadership of Joaquim do Amor Divino Rabelo e Caneca (1774–1825), Frei Caneca, stood out; the so-called Conjuração Baiana, between 1798

---

5. Antonio Paim, *História do Liberalismo Brasileiro* (LVM Editora, 2018), 48.

and 1799, which merged agendas such as the creating a republic and ending slavery, and which was supported by shoemakers, tailors, and former slaves; and the most notorious among them, Inconfidência Mineira (or Conjuração Mineira), in 1789. The last, occurring in the same year that the French Third Estate, in the meeting of the Estates-General, ignited the spark that cause the fire of French Revolution, mainly gathered leaders from the province of Minas Gerais, in collusion against the Portuguese Crown's colonial power.

The attraction of this displeased elite to the North American example may be ascertained through reference to the curious case known as the "Vendek Mission." In 1787, Thomas Jefferson (1743–1826) claimed to have received, in his role as United States ambassador to France, a letter signed with the pseudonym "Vendek" from a student at the University of Montpellier, who asked him to confidentially initiate contact. Welcoming the invitation, Jefferson acquired from Vendek the information that there were revolutionaries in Brazil who, inspired by the example of the United States, hoped to receive from the Northern nation material support in their revolt against the Portuguese Crown and its high taxes. "They consider the North American revolution as a precedent for theirs," Jefferson reported. "They look to the United States as most likely to give them honest support, and from a variety of considerations have the strongest prejudices in our favor. . . . In case of a succesful revolution, a republican government in a single body, would probably be established."[6] Though he expressed his sympathy toward this revolutionary aspiration, Jefferson did not pledge any support whatsoever, probably because the risk of inciting European powers wouldn't have been in the young American nation's best interest.

The 1776 North American example also inspired the processes of independence in other European countries' colonial possessions. In the early nineteenth century, the revolutionary idea that colonies no longer needed to serve the metropole's dictates was spread throughout the entirety of Hispanic America. The experience of the United States showed that the severance of political ties was not only possible but even advantageous. The wars of independence waged in the region between 1808 and 1829 resulted in the creation of several independent countries in the territory that had previously been governed by the Spanish, from Mexico to Argentina to Chile. Some leaders stood out for captaining such movements: among them Venezuelan Simón Bolívar (1783–1830) and Argentinian José de San Martín (1778–1850). To understand the nature of those wars of independence and the political regimes, often authoritarian, that succeeded them, it is necessary to recall the notable influence exerted by French-Swiss philosopher Jean-Jacques Rousseau in these movements, which

---

6. Thomas Jefferson, "From Thomas Jefferson to John Jay, 4 May 1787," *National Archives*. Available online at: https://founders.archives.gov/documents/Jefferson/01-11-02-0322.

gave rise to more radical positions, such as collectivist egalitarianism and democratism—in addition to the use of elements taken both from British liberal philosophy and the more successful facets of South Americans' own concrete historical experience.

In the specific case of Portuguese America, the process of emancipation was quite unique. Contrary to what is often believed, a great deal of bloodshed was involved, just as in the United States and the Hispanic colonies. Similar to what occurred in the United States, where leaders with various perspectives came together on a common axis, resulting in the institutional foundations of the American public life, the Brazilian project also brought together statesmen and engaged leaders with different conceptions. The main differences, however, lay in the factors which defined the common axis. In North America, the patriots' ideals converged toward the 1776 Declaration of Independence and the 1787 Constitution, albeit not without conflicts between the federalists—defenders of a larger central structure that would be somewhat autonomous from its component units—and the antifederalists—who advocated the maintenance of the system prior to the Constitution, wherein the United States had no presidents, national tax system, or national courts.

Lusitanian America was a far less educated society. Brazil's independence also had its textual trademarks, such as the Manifestos of August 1822 and the 1824 constitution itself, yet the main axis, as paradoxical as it seems to the republican mainstay around which the thirteen colonies aligned, was the heir of the House of Bragança, in the figure of Portugal's crown prince. The successful independence process in Brazil orbited around the image of Portuguese king João VI's heir, future Brazilian emperor Pedro I, who would also become Portuguese king Pedro IV, although he chose to forfeit the crown in 1826 in favor of his daughter Maria II—aside from having refused the Spanish and Greek crowns, which were offered to him due to his reputation as a devotee of liberal ideals.

After the events of the French Revolution from 1789 to 1799, as well as the imminence of a military invasion of Portugal by Napoleonic troops, as had occurred in Spain, King João VI's Portuguese court moved from Lisbon to Brazil, which turned the colonial territory into the actual center of the Portuguese Empire, a situation unparalleled in the New World colonies. In 1815, João VI raised Brazil's stature by establishing the United Kingdom of Portugal, Brazil, and Algarves, which subsequently created a relative sense of autonomy and unity in the population, without the kingdom severing its formal ties with its old metropole in Europe.

Several institutional and economic developments, such as the opening of the ports to friendly nations—thereby overthrowing the former colonial exclusivism— led to the Kingdom of Brazil being regarded as an even more thriving nation than its older sibling, Portugal. The Portuguese liberal revolution in 1820, having brought about constitutionalism and João VI's return to Portugal, was, however, contaminated by the perception of greater prosperity in Brazil and demanded actions that would lead to the dissolution of the sense of unity in the Kingdom of Brazil and to the fragmentation of power among the provinces, submitting some of them to the rule of military juntas commanded by the administration in Lisbon.

Some liberals in Brazil sympathized with the revolt's general goals. Liberalism, as inspired by England, found active representatives in Brazil in figures like journalist Hipólito José da Costa (1774–1823) and philosopher Silvestre Pinheiro Ferreira (1769–1846), among others. Nonetheless, the Portuguese constituents' sentiment regarding the relegation of Brazil to the condition of a mere Portuguese colony were reluctantly acknowledged even by Brazilian liberals. While Americans in 1776 rebelled against the creation of taxes without consent and the against postures assumed by the British courts that clashed with the interests of the colonists, Brazilians in 1822 rose against the threats made by the Portuguese constituent assembly, which, despite its liberal inspiration, proved to be anti-Brazilian. Brazilians rejected their parliamentarians' under-representation, the transfer of more Brazilian resources to Portugal, and the extinction of Brazil-based executive power and the higher spheres of judicial power, as all the main decisions would be transferred back to Lisbon.

The project of many of the Brazilian statesmen was to preserve the United Kingdom, but the succession of events convinced them to begin a gradual emancipation movement around the prince regent, future emperor Pedro I, who remained in Brazil after the departure of João VI as the representative of the Crown in the Kingdom of Brazil, contrary to the orders of Portuguese revolutionists. By the end of this process, the successful independence movement established a new monarchy, with Dom Pedro being proclaimed by the population as the first Brazilian emperor and definitively triumphed in 1823, in the aftermath of military conflicts, mainly in the northern and northeastern regions of the country, where there was more loyalty to the Portuguese government. The heir located in Brazil, following the historical experience of the Portuguese Court on Brazilian ground, was the institutional mainstay the leaders of the process needed in order to unify the movement and maintain Portuguese America as one, large, united empire, as opposed to what occurred in Hispanic America, which dissolved into several small republics.

Brazil was born a monarchy, whereas the United States was born a republic; nonetheless, the United States was among the first countries to politically acknowledge Brazil's independence, doing so in 1824, second after Argentina, which had recognized the new nation in 1823. This alacrity was due to the adherence of the United States to the so-called Monroe Doctrine, established by President James Monroe (1758–1831), who basically stood against any manifestations of European colonialism in the American continent.

The difference in form of government adopted by the United States and Brazil does not prevent us from identifying a series of pertinent parallels between some of the characters who featured in the births of the two nations. Throughout the American War of Independence, the leadership of George Washington (1732–1799), who was destined to become the first president of the new country, stood out, and his political prominence was equally decisive to assure the consolidation of the 1787 Constitution, which represented the triumph of federalists over anti-federalists. He feared that excessive decentralization would lead to chaos and the country's defensive fragility before potential invaders. Washington became the symbolic human backbone of the emerging nation, as he cultivated the rituals surrounding the institution of the presidency and made the path of greater centralization, which was what the federalists wanted, prevail, without eroding the autonomy of the states. Washington was even accused of intending to create a monarchy but, aware of the particular basis on which the United States had been grounded, he never exhibited such a tendency. He owned slaves and was never strongly opposed to slavery, but there are indications in his biography that he gradually came to acknowledge just how objectionable that labor system was. In many respects, the first president of the United States may be regarded as a model of the nation's conservatism.

In the Brazilian context, Emperor Pedro I may be compared to George Washington, albeit with a few obvious differences. Among them there is the fact that he was always averse to slavery and never personally had slaves, not to mention that he was a monarch. Born on October 12, 1798, in Queluz's National Palace, Portugal, Dom Pedro was but nine years old when his family left for Brazil. His personality was deemed highly self-willed, and the ending of his time as Brazilian monarch wasn't particularly joyous, in contrast with Washington's peaceful farewell from the presidency of the United States. The emperor went so far as to dissolve the 1823 Brazilian Constituent Assembly, even though it is important to acknowledge that the general aspects of the constitution legitimated by him in 1824 stemmed from it. Nonetheless, as a king, his belief in the inevitability of the liberal agenda—what he called "new ideas"—is notable. The thought of the first Brazilian emperor was influenced by French-Swiss philosopher and liberal activist Benjamin Constant de Rebecque (1767–1830), and Neapolitan jurist Caetano Filangieri (1753–1788), who argued that the old feudal European principles had caused misery in Europe and that the monarchic elites themselves should lead "orderly revolutions" that would establish the assurance of individual rights. His worldview was also shaped by his reading of Irish philosopher and statesman Edmund Burke, regarded by many as the "father of modern conservatism," given his eloquent criticism to the French Revolution as well as his political ideas. Pedro I neither sought the complete abolition of existing traditions nor displayed an excessive attachment to the absolutist past. He found in these liberal authors, tempered by conservative cautions, the theoretical inspiration to reform political institutions. The monarchic constitution established the three traditional powers (executive, legislative, and judicial), plus the moderating power—inspired by the work of Benjamin Constant and exclusive to the emperor—which was the subject of endless debate throughout the whole imperial period. The country discarded the practice of lifetime senators chosen by the emperor from a list of three candidates proposed by the voters. Representatives in the new senate instead would be selected by popular vote. Catholicism remained the state's official religion.

Concerning the Brazilian Constitution, even before it was written, Pedro I described what he expected from the document:

A wise, just, and enforceable constitution, governed by reason rather than by whim, intending nothing but general happiness, which can never be great without such a constitution having solid foundations, foundations which the wisdom of the centuries has proved to be truthful, in order to grant the peoples rightful liberty and all due strength to the executive power. A constitution wherein the three powers are well-divided, in a way that they cannot arrogate rights that do not concern them, yet that are organized and harmonized in a such a manner that it becomes impossible, even in the course of time, for enemies to me made, so that they act, hand in hand, in favor of the state's overall happiness. In short, a constitution that, by putting up inaccessible barriers to despotism, whether royal or aristocratic, scares off anarchy and plants the seeds of the freedom under whose shadow union, tranquility, and the independence of this empire must grow, which shall awe the new and old worlds.[7]

---

7. Otávio Tarquínio de Sousa, *A Vida de D. Pedro I – História dos Fundadores do Império do Brasil: Volume II* (Senado Federal, 2015), 464.

One cannot fail to acknowledge the similarities between such a description and the concerns voiced by the United States' founding fathers. In the United States, where the associative and community spirit had previously developed in each of the colonies, their union in response to the British Crown generated a republic. In Brazil, on the other hand, with a more anemic development of such associative spirit and more obstacles to social and territorial integration, where society was accustomed to a unity rooted in the very Crown that lay at its core and whose enemies were the Portuguese who wanted to displace it, the path toward founding an empire was taken. The spirit of balancing order and liberty without fully breaking with the beacons of the historical-cultural past and the values inspired by it was nonetheless present in both cases, and it animated both George Washington and Pedro I.

Unfortunately, the emperor's temper and his Lusitanian roots sparked profound resistance in society, which culminated in his forfeiting the crown on April 7, 1831. Subsequently, however, the first Brazilian emperor proved to be decisive in the history of Portugal, as he led the opposition to the resumption of absolutism by his brother Miguel I, who usurped the throne from his niece, Maria II, who, thanks to her father's military actions, managed to get it back. Much like he had previously done in Brazil, Pedro I bestowed, in 1826, a liberal constitution on Portugal, which remained in force until 1910, when a republican coup overthrew the Portuguese regime. As a result of injuries sustained in combat, Pedro I passed away at the young age of thirty-four, on September

24, 1834, in the same bed in which he had been born, in the Palace of Queluz.

Also famous among the founding fathers of the United States, John Adams (1735–1826), the nation's second president, despite having taken part in the process of independence, was devoted to mitigating anti-British feeling among the population of the new nation and to preserving the old rights earned in British tradition. An extremely erudite man, well-versed in the Greco-Roman classics, Adams accepted belatedly, compared to the other founding fathers, the need of an armed revolt and political separation. According to Russell Kirk's analysis, Adams's conservatism had to do with two radicalisms:

> one of French origins, the same enormous social and intellectual convulsion that Burke confronted; the other a growth in part native and in part English, the levelling agrarian republicanism of which [Thomas] Jefferson was the chief representative, anxious to abolish entail, primogeniture, church establishments, and all the vestiges of aristocracy, and to oppose centralization, strong government, state debt, and the military.[8]

---

8. Russell Kirk, *Conservative Mind: From Burke to Eliot*, 7th ed. (Regnery Publishing, 1986), 72-73.

Like Edmund Burke and other conservatives, Adams believed in the need for religious belief in order to sustain society, in practical considerations over abstract theory, in the contrast between human beings' imperfect nature and the doctrines of systematic philosophers, and in the importance of balanced government.[9] Moreover, he argued that there existed a natural aristocracy, as, even though everyone is born with equal rights, there are always differences and, consequently, leaderships. Although closer to the Federalists, Adams was not in perfect alignment with any political faction.

The aforementioned José da Silva Lisboa, Viscount of Cairu, paralleled Adams in the foundation of the Brazilian motherland. Cairu may be seen as even more Burkean than the North American statesman, since he referred in a more extensive and enthusiastic manner to the Irish philosopher and statesman's work. He was the foremost proponent of Burke's thought in the Portuguese language, as he organized, translated, and prefaced several of his Burke's writings, just as he was responsible for the dissemination of the economic works of Adam Smith (1723–1790) and Jean-Baptiste Say (1767–1832), as well as those of other important European authors associated with liberalism. Highly valued by generations as the first Brazilian economist, Cairu was born in Salvador, in the state of Bahia, son of a Portuguese father and a Bahian mother. Much like Adams greatly appreciated the maintenance of

---

9. Kirk, *Conservative Mind*, 88.

concord between the United States and England, Cairu defended as much as he could the continuity of the United Kingdom of Portugal, Brazil and Algaves. He was equally erudite, a connoisseur of Latin grammar at a mere eight years of age, the beneficiary of philosophical studies under the guidance of Bahian Carmelites, and a student of music, especially piano. Later studying law at the University of Coimbra, Cairu was versed in scholastic philosophy and was a profoundly religious man and a vocal critic of Masonry. On this point, Cairu was markedly different from almost all the founding fathers of the United States, considering the importance of Masonic lodges in the country, but he also diverged from most of the other founding fathers of Brazil, given that the same was true in the South American nation.

Cairu got a double bachelor's degree in law and philosophy at the age of twenty-three and came back to Brazil, having taught Greek, Hebrew, and philosophy, as well as practicing law. He showed great interest in economics, and he analyzed work relations in Bahia and criticized the governing slave-labor regime in Brazil. Serving in several public offices, he became a relevant figure in the courts of both João VI and Pedro I, despite holding no ministerial posts. He was a fervent supporter of monarchic and Catholic tradition, and he despised the French Revolution and Jacobinism. Thus he defined his position regarding Brazilian independence just fifteen days before Pedro I's definitive gesture: "I have cordially longed for the union between Brazil and Portugal, and, as much as I could, I have made literary efforts for them to be in concordance, but now I see that I have done so in vain: all the illusions have dissipated, and almost all the hopes of reconciliation have vanished."[10] In 1821, however, he protested against the Lisboner customs, denouncing the presence of what he called an "anti-Brazilian cabal" among Portuguese liberals. As a parliamentarian, he was opposed to federalism and decentralization, as well as an enemy of all revolutions and an ardent defender of the 1824 constitution and, especially, of the monarchy. Combining aspects of modernization proposals embraced in the University of Coimbra with the British liberal economic agenda and rhetoric inspired by feudalism and traditionalism, Cairu's mentality was an understandable synthesis within a man who had lived through a time of transition. In both Adams and Cairu, we find a recognition of the inevitability of aristocracy, a reverence for tradition, and an appreciation of continuity.

At the head of the opposition to federalist centralization in the United States was Thomas Jefferson, the third president of the United States. A versatile man, possessing talents as an intellectual, politician, architect, statesman, diplomat, jurist, and philosopher, Jefferson maintained a rocky relationship of both friendship and political rivalry with John Adams. The main author of the Declaration of Independence, Jefferson stressed the theoretical dimension of his agenda in defense of liberty, directly inspired by French Enlightenment philosophers such as Mon-

---

10. Elysio de Oliveira Belchior, *Visconde de Cairu: Vida e Obra* (Confederação Nacional do Comércio, 2000), 108.

tesquieu (1689–1755) and Voltaire (1694–1778), as well as the Lockean tradition. He promoted rural life and the greatest possible autonomy for the American states, opposing the expansion of the central government, though he did advocate the presence of the state in education, for instance. He sympathized with the thrust of the French Resolution, though rejecting its bloodier and more totalitarian consequences. Deeply leery of authority and disconnected from the etiquette and formal traditions of the institution of the presidency, Jefferson took a keen interest in science, in general, including botany, cartography, mineralogy, astronomy, and navigation—thus he kept in his library a vast collection of maps and works on the natural history of the United States. He was a known enthusiast of education and knowledge as the pillars of a promising, stable nation, and he was himself an inventor, helping to conceive and improve minor technologies that were innovative for his time.

Another major figure among the founding fathers of the United States was Benjamin Franklin (1706–1790), a true polymath, oriented toward scientific experiments and inventions, dedicated to encouraging the dissemination of the discoveries made by men of science. Franklin served the colonies and new nation with his diplomatic abilities especially. He became, several years after independence, a staunch supporter of the abolition of slavery. Deistic, yet an advocate for the utility of organized religions, he believed in the importance of virtue in the core of society as a base on which republican institutions were to sit.

The character that is most similar, simultaneously, to Jefferson and Franklin in the Brazilian situation—and who has been compared to both—was José Bonifácio de Andrada e Silva (1763–1838), known in Brazil as the Patriarch of Independence. Concerning Jefferson in particular, there are some notable differences to point out. Whereas Jefferson favored a more radically decentralizing movement, Bonifácio leaned toward the necessity of a higher degree of centralization within the Brazilian context. While Jefferson's relationship with slavery was ambiguous, given that he kept slaves and was considered one of the most reluctant among the founding fathers to deal with the subject (though he defended gradual abolition), Bonifácio was the staunchest enemy of slavery out of all Brazil's founders, which certainly contributed to reducing his political influence during the first days of the independent empire. Even so, there remain good reasons for the analogy between the two.

José Bonifácio was born in Santos, in the state of São Paulo, into a traditional family. At first, he was educated in his homeland by his parents and local priests, but he finished his studies in the University of Coimbra. An enthusiast of books and knowledge, he came into contact, in Portugal, with liberal and Enlightenment literature. While Cairu utterly rejected them, Rousseau's works somewhat interested Bonifácio, as did the works of Voltaire—the latter more intensely. Nonetheless, he did not draw from them any appreciation for radical rebellion or democratic extremism. He much preferred living in a monarchy that was influenced by Enlightenment ideals, pruned of despotic excesses, versus the rule of the masses that would be perennially revolutionary rather than reformist. Bonifácio's fondness for traditional institutions, such as monarchy, was mainly utilitarian rather than ideological; he admired inventors and "doers" a lot more than monarchs and public authorities in general. As a mineralogist and renowned scientist, Bonifácio traveled through Europe as a researcher, and so came into contact with notable intellectuals of the Old World and joined various scientific societies. In Portugal, he fought against French invaders in 1807, thence returning to Brazil, at the age of fifty-six, eager to work for the technical-scientific and economic growth of his kingdom of birth. When the revolutionary convulsion arose in Portugal in the 1820s, Bonifácio became Emperor Pedro I's close counselor, as well as one of the main leaders of the independence movement. He worried, simultaneously, about maintaining the unity of Portuguese America and avoiding a revolutionary waywardness that would be similar to the chaos in France. He was fueled by a desire for Brazil to become a kingdom grounded on the cultivation of knowledge and enlightenment. However, Bonifácio transcended such worries, for he also wished to build a multicultural nation that would provide solidity for Brazilian institutions by blending into the European element the native and African elements. He was vehement in condemning slavery and devised a gradual abolition plan that was meant to lessen the slaves' suffering and, had his plan been followed, would have abolished that oppressive institution earlier than actually occurred. Bonifácio believed the ethnic mix would make Brazil a new civilization, an amalgamation of advantages that would cultivate harmony through the differences. Of the Brazilian people, he diagnosed and predicted the following:

> They are enthusiasts of such a beautiful ideal, friends of their freedom, and barely grieve over losing the perks they were once given. Obedient to the just, enemies of the arbitrary, they accept stealing better than vilification; ignorant due to lack of instruction, yet naturally filled with talent and a brilliant imagination, thus sympathetic toward novelties that hold promises of perfection and ennoblement; generous, but with bravado; capable of great deeds, so long as they do not require accurate attention and diligent, monotonous work; passionate about sex due to weather, life, and education. They engage in a lot of endeavors, yet conclude but a handful of them; they are America's Athenians, as long as they are not constricted and tyrannized by despotism.[11]

Interestingly enough, on April 22, 1955, a statue of José Bonifácio was installed in Bryant Park in New York City, in a joint initiative taken by the United States Department of State and the Brazilian government. On that occasion, Brazilian ambassador

---

11. José Bonifácio de Andrada e Silva, *Projetos para o Brasil*, (Companhia das Letras, 2000), 97.

João Carlos Muniz (1893–1960) compared Bonifácio precisely to the figures of Thomas Jefferson and Benjamin Franklin.[12]

The list of founders, both of Brazil and the United States, is much longer than this brief presentation has indicated. However, it seems fit to stop here in order to more fully illustrate the diversity among the statesmen who were leading figures in both processes, by mentioning the least conservative constituents in the nations' emergence. In the United States, Thomas Paine (1737–1809), born in England, was one of the most influential pamphleteers among American patriots. Yet he was extremely critical of George Washington's actions, of organized religion, and of Edmund Burke's conservatism, allying with the Girondins during the French Revolution. In this respect, he could be compared to the most extreme faction within the Brazilian emancipationist process, represented by the Freemasons of the state of Rio de Janeiro, whose main leader was Joaquim Gonçalves Ledo (1781–1847), editor of the newspaper *Revérbero Constitucional Fluminense*. Despite being a member of the elite, he counted on pedagogical and pamphleteer efforts to mobilize people and raise awareness. Even though some of Rio de Janeiro's Masons were fond of the idea of a republic, they also understood that the concrete circumstances demanded the presence of King Pedro I so that

---

12. See "Um santista na Big Apple," available online at: https://memoriasantista.com.br/santista-jose-bonifacio-de-andrada-tem-estatua-inaugurada-em-nova-iorque-em-1955/.

independence would be achieved. The difference was that Ledo and his peers nurtured more urgent yearnings for a constitutional convention than, for instance, José Bonifácio or Cairu, who sought, first, to reinforce the emperor's authority, fearing as they did the possibility that events like those in France might occur in Brazil. While a student in Portugal, Ledo refused to fight against the French invaders (unlike Bonifácio), for he already deemed the Kingdom of Portugal an oppressor of Brazil. In the year 1822, having called for the implementation of an independent empire, he claimed that "nature did not create satellites that are larger than their respective planets. America should belong to America, Europe to Europe, for it was not in vain that the Great Architect of the Universe shoved between them the enormous amount of space which separates them from one another."[13]

---

13. Nicola Aslan, *Biografia de Joaquim Gonçalves Ledo*, vol. 2 (Editora Maçônica, 1947), 227-236.

4

CROWNED LIBERALISM AND REPUBLICAN REVOLUTION

The Brazilian personalities mentioned in the previous chapter, like other prominent figures in the national pantheon, assured the birth of the Brazilian Empire, which went through three stages during its historical development. The initial epoch was the so-called First Reign, between the years 1822 and 1831, when, despite several internal conflicts, Pedro I and his collaborators introduced some of the country's institutional foundations, merging the traditional monarchic heritage with modern liberal ideas. Afterward, from Pedro I's renunciation in 1831 until Pedro II was declared of legal age in 1840, there was the turbulent time of the Regency, when the country was governed by a succession of regents, which was in some ways a sort of republican experience. Finally, Brazil was plunged into the Second Reign, when Pedro II ascended to the throne and ruled for fifty-eight years, the most institutionally stable period in Brazilian history. Throughout these three stages, the Constitution of 1824 prevailed, with some modifications along the way. The 1834 Additional Act (equivalent to a constitutional amendment) was instituted during the Regency epoch, a single great reform bringing a few substantial changes in favor of large-scale decentralization—many of them reversed by the so-called Regress, which marks the emergence of conservative tendencies.

Throughout the Regency, various separatist rebellions broke out, threatening the nation's unity. These included Cabanagem in Grão-Pará (1832–1840); Sabinada in Bahia (1837–1838); Balaiada in Maranhão (1838–1841); and the Ragamuffin War in Rio Grande do Sul (1835–1845). Aside from the firm military intervention during the imperial government, the insurrections were contained via two fundamental political acts.

The first element responsible for national pacification was the movement of Regress, initiated in 1837, which opposed the strong regency of the priest Diogo Antônio Feijó (1784–1843) and proposed to moderate the decentralizing excesses that had encouraged diverse separatist uprisings. The Regress movement was led by journalist, magistrate, and parliamentarian Bernardo Pereira de Vasconcelos (1795–1850), whose actions were influenced by the tradition of liberalism, in both its Lockean British and doctrinaire French aspects, by some of the political ideas of Thomas Hobbes (1588–1679) and Alexander Hamilton (1757–1804), and by the Burkean counterrevolutionary mentality. The movement aimed to restore the principles of monarchic authority, and the result was the foundation in 1837 of the Regressive Party, which in 1848 changed its name to the Party of Order and finally, from 1853, adopted the name Conservative Party, which it retained until 1889, when it was annihilated by the republican military coup.

The second driving force behind Brazil's pacification was the movement conducted by the Liberal Party that encouraged popular unrest in favor of anticipation by the parliament of Pedro II's coming of age. Thus, instead having to await age twenty-one, as stipulated by the 1824 Constitution, Pedro ascended to the throne in 1840 at the age of fourteen, assuring the nation's political stability. Beloved by most of his subjects due to his prudent conduct of national policies, his promotion of culture as patron of the arts, and his support for technological and scientific advancements, the second Brazilian emperor was also greatly respected internationally, taking several trips abroad—paid from his personal finances rather than the public treasury—as well as maintaining extensive correspondence with renowned foreign intellectuals. He was the first monarch to visit the lands of the robust North American Republic, traveling to the United States in 1876 during the centennial of American independence. Over the course of the excursion, he became acquainted with scientist, inventor, and engineer Alexander Graham Bell (1847–1922), and was persuaded to buy shares in his pioneering phone company. The records of this visit show that thousands of American citizens wrote the name of Pedro II on their election ballot, even though the Brazilian emperor obviously was not one of the candidates for the presidency of the United States.[1]

At that time, the American nation fluctuated between its founders' original distrust regarding political factions, which would come to be characteristic in all developing representative systems throughout the nineteenth century, and a variety of divisions that were in fact emerging. From the division between federalists and antifederalists there developed the rivalry between Federalists and Democratic-Republicans. In 1828, while Pedro I still ruled in Brazil, the Democratic-Republican Party, which had vanquished the Federalists, was itself split, giving rise to the Whig Party, a coalition that advocated the strengthening of Congress and the action of the state to promote industrial and economic growth, whereas the Democrats organized themselves around the agenda of the president's supremacy, the maintenance of low taxes, and a preference for the interests of farmers. The slavery issue gained momentum during the 1850s in the United States, when Pedro II was Emperor of Brazil, which brought about the strengthening of an anti-slavery faction within the Whig Party (already on its way toward extinction), from which the Republican Party would emerge. It goes without saying that, since both liberal and con-

---

1. See Gustavo Schneider, "The Brazilian Emperor That The USA Loved," *Medium*, October 29, 2017, https://medium.com/@Gustavoschneider1/the-brazilian-emperor-usa-loved-cb3641d1e84c.

servative ideas, principles, and values inspired and molded North American society, the term "liberal" in the United States, without ever having referred to a specific party, became more closely associated with a progressive and statist political view, especially during the twentieth century, thus straying far from the legacy left by classic liberals. Meanwhile, the term "conservative" rose to popularity in the decade of 1840, when personalities such as John C. Calhoun (1782–1850), Daniel Webster (1782–1852), and Orestes Brownson (1803–1876) employed it—although they held different positions amid the political infighting of the time.

Imperial Brazilian politics was closer to the British parliamentary system. The group composing the so-called "moderate liberals," advocates of territorial unity and constitutional monarchy, triumphed in the Regency's political conflicts and became dominant in the Second Reign, splitting into the Liberal Party and the Conservative Party, the members of each becoming known, respectively, by the pejorative monikers "*luzias*" and "*saquaremas.*"

During the term of the Brazilian parliamentary system, which lasted for forty-two years, hegemony belonged to the conservatives. The *saquaremas* remained in power for a total of twenty-seven years, in fifteen distinct cabinets, with eleven different presidents. Having held chief positions in the imperial state for mere fifteen years, the *luzias* led seventeen cabinets, including the three in the so-called Progressive League, with a total of thirteen different presidents. The liberal association took over the ministerial presidency in four separate but consecutive moments: from 1847 to 1848, from 1862 to 1868, from 1878 to 1885, and, finally, in 1889, including the first and last imperial cabinets. At three specific times, from 1848 to 1862, from 1868 to 1878, and from 1885 to 1889, the *saquaremas* presided over ministries, which provided Brazil with the second-most solid, organized, and self-aware political basis, behind only the United Kingdom itself.

In general, both liberals and conservatives represented distinct internal branches of moderate liberalism, which rejected the left wing's revolutionary egalitarian and anarchic radicalism and the right wing's reactionary authoritarianism. The two factions, each in their own way, were influenced by the example provided by the United States, since both *luzias* and *saquaremas* acknowledged the importance of studying the successes achieved and the storms faced by the giant nation, which shared the same hemisphere with Brazil as well as the condition of being a colossus within the New World.

One of the main theorists and leaders of the Conservative Party, jurist, magistrate, and parliamentarian Paulino José Soares de Sousa (1807–1866), Viscount of Uruguay, in his work *Ensaio sobre o Direito Administrativo* (An Essay on Administrative Law), compared the administrative experiences in countries such as France, England, and the United States to the one in Brazil, which he regarded as a young nation that needed to derive inspiration from other models and traditions in order to engineer some of its institutions, while acclimating these models to the Brazilian sociocultural context. Conservatives from the monarchic period believed in the pertinence, allowing for the peculiarities of context, of institutions like the lifetime senate, the council of state, the monarch's moderating power, and political centralization, with the possibility of the emperor acting over the provinces through the province presidents (who are now equivalent to state governors), appointed by the central government.

The main rationale for this approach was the fact that imperial elections would be affected by the absence of the development of community spirit and self-government among Brazilians, when compared to other societies, and, furthermore, the lack of separation between demographic concentrations and the dominance of local political partialities over the political machine, hence suffocating the opposition. In this regard, besides the concrete experience of British parliamentarism and Alexander Hamilton's view on American institutions, politicians such as the Viscount of Uruguay were heavily influenced by the ideas of Benjamin Constant and Alexis de Tocqueville, prominent representatives of the French liberal tradition. However, Brazilian conservatives were also guided by the so-called French doctrinaires. Taking historian and statesman François Guizot (1787–1874) as an example, the doctrinaires embraced a certain reinforcement of authority and tighter voting restrictions. The Viscount of Uruguay claimed that in the United States administrative functions were quite decentralized, which depended on educational levels and special habits that had been developed during the colonial period. According to his diagnosis,

> We have inherited the Portuguese monarchy's centralization. When independence came, alongside the

constitution that governs us, we left behind the administration of captain-generals, magistrates of the districts, providers, *juízes-de-fora* ["outsider judges"] and ordinaries, *almotacés*, ordination chambers. . . . We did not provide for an education that practically enabled us to govern ourselves, like the one the British had been enforcing for centuries and which was inherited by the United States; we could not have acquired the habits and the practical sense such a system demanded. The most forward men concerning liberal ideas had gotten them by drinking from the more exaggerated fountains and tended to take as a model the institutions of the United States, which, to them, was the purest and most genuine expression of liberalism. On the other hand, the men called to power showed tendencies of conserving what already existed, what they had studied and known, in lieu of advancing just and reasonable practical reforms, accommodated to the nation's circumstances, that would perform the transition.[2]

Regardless of their profound knowledge of theoretical sources, the action of the *saquaremas*, first and foremost, was inspired, as

---

2. Paulino José Soares de Souza, *Ensaio sobre o Direito Administrativo* (Typographia Nacional, 1862), 163.

noted, in the concrete examples of the United States and England. In his assessment of the topic, the Viscount of Uruguay stated the following:

> The English immigrants who founded the United States brought with them the spirit of those (British) institutions, education, and the required habits to handle them. Born, as Tocqueville points out, in a country that was, throughout centuries, agitated by the clash between parties, wherein factions had been forced, each in turn, to put themselves under the provision of the laws, their political education had taken place in such a rough school, and, among them, there lay spilled more notions of law and more principles of true liberty than in most European nations. At the time of the first immigrations, the city government, a fruitful seed of the free institutions, was already profoundly ingrained in English habits, and with it the dogma concerning the people's sovereignty had indeed been introduced in the Tudors' monarchy.... The colonies there (America) carried the seed of a full-on democracy. Almost all the immigrants came from the middle class and had no estimate of superiority over others.... Such admirable immigrants brought with them elements of order and morality.... The different states of the American Union were isolated from one another, under the

> rule of the colonial government, and each had its own separate government. Having earned, through independence, their individual sovereignty, they did not consent to being absorbed into the collective union. These sovereignties coexist without being mistaken for one another, and it is anything but easy to determine with due accuracy where one ends and the other begins.[3]

Without disregarding the fruitful experiences Brazilian administrators might learn from the American nation, the Viscount of Uruguay and his allies stressed the need to look at the great social and cultural differences between the United States and Brazil, which would impose substantial modifications upon the enforcement of any prescription in the South American empire. The *saquaremas'* emphasis on the need to adapt foreign ideas and institutions to the concrete reality of their own country, which the Viscount of Uruguay called a "clarified eclecticism," was grounded on the ideal of "primacy of circumstance," in contrast to the idealism of most *luzias*.

Unlike the *saquaremas*, with their centralizing position, the main leaders and theorists bound to the Liberal Party usually defended the extinction of the state council and the lifetime senate, as well as the need of a ministerial countersignature to the actions

---

3. Souza, *Ensaio sobre o Direito Administrativo*, 174-175.

taken by the moderating power, and they advocated federalism, which would grant a larger degree of autonomy to the provinces. Liberal authors such as lawyer, journalist, and parliamentarian Aureliano Tavares Bastos (1839–1875) saw, in centralization, a retrograde political practice to be unconditionally fought against in all its aspects, as it was regarded as having been mobilized by men lacking faith in America's providential mission and the destinies of democracy. Therefore, his attachment to the Anglo-Saxon example was even more strident, deploring France as a bad example in nearly every way. Tavares Bastos proposed the establishment in Brazil of a federation akin to the North American model, which would concede broad freedom and autonomy to the Brazilian provinces. As opposed to conservatives, who sought a gradual preparation of society for the coexistence of larger concessions of autonomy and institutions that were necessarily more centralized from a political standpoint—despite the Viscount of Uruguay's desire a certain administrative decentralization—Bastos wanted the people to immediately learn from the experience of living under those institutions whose flowering in Brazilian reality was dreamed of. Yet, he also acknowledged the existence of a past as the basis for the development of freedom and political participation in the United States, which can be seen in the following passage:

> Incidentally, American democracy did not consecrate an entirely new principle; humanity saw it into effect in the first free peoples mentioned by history, in Greek republics, and in Rome; then it was seen,

as it still is, in modern Europe and England themselves, wherefrom Puritan immigrants transported it to America.[4]

Conservatives and liberals—both, as we've seen, offspring of the "moderate liberals"—had different internal factions, more or less antithetical, more or less akin, which in general reconciled themselves in supporting a constitutional monarchic system, allowing for elections and, in practice, tolerating for decades the labor regime based on slavery. The conservative governments, nonetheless, which were the majority throughout the empire, slowly and successfully approved laws meant to eliminate slavery altogether, until its complete extinction in 1888. Abolitionism, a more intense defense of such extinction throughout the empire's last decades, was a cross-party movement, gathering abolitionist liberals and conservatives against pro-slavery liberals and conservatives. Even though the extinguishment of slavery took a lot longer than in the United States, where it was abolished in 1863, in Brazil the process did not depend on a bloody civil war but was instead the product of a political agenda programmed by the political elite itself, having also yielded to international pressures. Moreover, although the existence of racism in Brazil is undeniable, the Latin American country, due to miscegenation (see chapter 2), was not subjected to

---

4. Aureliano Cândido Tavares Bastos, *A Província: Estudo sobre a descentralização do Brasil* (B. L. Garnier, 1870), 49.

the troubling laws regarding racial segregation that were enforced in the United States for much of the twentieth century.

Furthermore, there existed within the Brazilian Empire, from the 1870s on, the Republican Party, which overtly stood for the extinction of monarchy in the nation without suffering from any sort of censorship by the imperial government. The republican movement gained momentum in the state of São Paulo from a group of liberal professionals and farmers who advocated European immigration, to replace the slave workforce, and the maintenance of more resources in the hands of the provinces during the time of economic problems stemming from the Paraguayan War, during which the Brazilian Empire from 1864 to 1870 fought alongside Uruguay and Argentina against the neighboring republic. It coexisted, however, with a certain ambiguity concerning the problem of slavery, since the Republican Party was not unanimous about it.

Unlike what occurred in the United States, the implementation of a republic in Brazil occurred on November 15, 1889, through a military coup. The republican government in Brazil gathered liberal forces of different tendencies, positivists—influenced, in various ways by the philosophy of Frenchman August Comte (1798–1857)—and members of the military who were more or less extreme, the more radical ones known as "Jacobins" and inspired by French revolutionaries. Despite the fact that the ideas of order, value, and liberty were embraced by the founders of both nations, the United States underwent the various moments of their history under the aegis of the same 1787Constitution and founding regime. By means of a traumatic rupture, which set off, within the republican cycle, a succession of subsequent ruptures, Brazil forfeited the 1824 Constitution and the original monarchic regime.

In the United States, the opposition between the Republican Party and the Democratic Party was cemented, with the former, from the 1890s on, predominating, as it implemented a larger role for the state within society, with an increase in governmental regulation of taxes, labor laws, and trade union activity, and also introducing the vote for women—a period known as "Progressive Era." During the same period, a republic ruled by military authoritarianism arose in Brazil, and later, a civil oligarchic government took its place, separating Church and state and implementing a fragile federalism, which "functioned" thanks to the extremely restricted vote and to a pact between the president of the republic and the state elites, which severely hindered alternations of power. The influence of liberal currents on the elaboration of the 1891 Constitution, nonetheless, managed to prevent positivist and militarist currents from taking over the nation.

The freedom of religion erected by the republic, supported in speeches delivered by polymath Rui Barbosa (1849–1923), was largely inspired by the secular system in place in the United States. While dismantling the confessional state, the republican secular state, according to Rui Barbosa, should not be anti-religious:

> I have written and preached against the consortium of the Church with the State since 1876; but I never

did it in the name of irreligion, but rather in the name of freedom. Why, freedom and religion are partners, not enemies. There is no religion without freedom. There is no freedom without religion.[5]

The presidential system and the federative form of organization were officially adopted in Brazil, even though in reality they faced the previously mentioned adversities. Brazilian Republicans believed Brazil ought to be a republic, like all the other countries within the American continent, especially the United States. This inspiration was so powerful that the nation's official name, until 1968, was the United States of Brazil. Other Republicans, more influenced by the authoritarian theses of French positivism, hoped that strengthening the executive power might bring Brazil closer to the ideal of the "republican dictatorship" they aimed to establish. In the words of jurist and philosopher Nelson Saldanha (1933–2015),

> Having lacked a past of actual autonomy, wherein each was an independent territory (as it is assumed in classic federations such as the United States and Switzerland), the new states did not properly know

---

5. Quoted in Thiago Rafael Vieira, *Liberdade Religiosa: Fundamentos teóricos para proteção e exercício da crença* (Almedina, 2023), 186.

what to do with the powers they had been granted. Furthermore, such powers, which should have been theirs to begin with, rather than given to them, would be slowly and gradually taken away by the Union, in the subsequent evolution of the country. ... One might say ... that federalism, which lived up to the complaints of several liberal generations, and which had been conceived by Rui Barbosa, was never fully put into practice in Brazil, being mistaken, at that point with local caciquism and criticized in the name of a greater political "efficiency."[6]

The institutional evolution during the first years of the Brazilian Republic hence show that Brazilians appreciated the North American experience yet mistook just how much they could draw inspiration from it and adapt it to a scenario filled with similarities but also quite a few differences—after all, all nations are exceptional when compared to others. Committed monarchist, lawyer, and journalist Eduardo Prado (1860–1901), author of *A Ilusão Americana* (The American Illusion), released in 1893, criticized the feeble attempt to faithfully reproduce the institutions of the United States within the Brazilian context, as well as the establishment of an automatic and rather naïve alignment between both

---

6. Nelson Saldanha, *O Pensamento Político no Brasil* (Editora Forense, 1978), 109-110.

countries. Nonethelsss, the rise of the Brazilian Old Republic was contemporary to the pan-Americanist movement, promoted by none other than the United States, which nurtured an idea of cooperation and fraternity among the nations of the American continent. One of the main sympathizers of pan-Americanism in Brazil, oddly enough, was notorious monarchist and abolitionist Joaquim Nabuco (1849–1910), accompanied by the pragmatic support of illustrious José Maria da Silva Paranhos Júnior (1845–1912), Baron of Rio Branco, a monarchist and protagonist, between 1902 and 1912, of Brazilian diplomacy. Nabuco decidedly adhered to the Monroe Doctrine, acknowledging Latin American countries' need to accept the northern republic's natural leadership in safeguarding their interests. Historian and diplomat Manuel de Oliveira Lima (1867–1928), whose library can be found in the Catholic University of America and whose human remains lie in Mount Olivet Cemetery in Washington, DC, was also a great admirer of the United States, even stating that Brazilians had a lot to learn from North Americans. By the end of his career, however, he did become quite critical of the possibility of any automatic alignment, advocating an adaptation of the Monroe Doctrine in the form of a "Latin-Americanized pan-Americanism" that mitigated the prevalence of the United States.

Still during the epoch of the Old Republic, roiled by revolts by junior military officers against the oligarchic government—part of a diffuse movement known as Tenentism—it is worth noting the figure of liberal theorist João Arruda (1861–1943), who published in 1927 the book *Do Regime Democrático* (On the democratic regime), in which he used as an epigraph, right at its beginning, "The price of freedom is eternal vigilance," by American founding father Patrick Henry (1736–1799). This motto would be taken up in the postwar period by the Brazilian liberals gathered at the *União Democrática Nacional* (National Democratic Union).

Before the emergence of that political party, however, the world underwent the painful decade of the 1930s, which was quite hostile toward the classic and conservative liberal order's agenda. With liberal institutions and the free market economy under attack across the globe, the United States witnessed the rise of the Democratic Party under the aegis of Franklin Delano Roosevelt (1882–1945), forming the political coalition of the New Deal, whose agenda emphasized the expansion of the government through an increase in public services, social insurance, and state intervention in the economy. Governing as president from 1933 to 1945, Roosevelt frequently clashed with the Supreme Court in his efforts to centralize power and expand the reach of government. Gradually, the forces opposed to the New Deal, especially from 1960 onward, coalesced in the Republican Party, which initiated a bipartisan political configuration similar to the one in evidence nowadays. This reaction, defeated, in 1964 in the candidacy of Republican Barry Goldwater (1909–1998), would come to triumph in 1980 with the victory of Ronald Reagan (1911–2004), who became a role model for classical liberal and conservative activists everywhere.

A crucial reference point for the emerging Brazilian "New Right," North American conservatives were reinvigorated and became more self-aware as a political phenomenon in the period after World War II, a rebirth that involved, according to the analysis made by historian George H. Nash, a coalition of three main forces.[7] The first was constituted by libertarians, heirs of individualistic criticisms made by authors such as Albert Jay Nock (1870–1945) and Isabel Paterson (1886–1961), who organized mainly around the ideas of Austrian philosopher and economist Friedrich August von Hayek (1899–1992). Hayek provided the intellectual foundation for the foundation during the postwar period of the Mont Pelerin Society, the institution responsible for assembling intellectuals and activists from across the world for the purpose of promoting classical liberal and libertarian ideas, in opposition to the excesses committed by "social liberalism" or "progressivism," which was ascendant in the United States, as well as to social democracy and the various forms of totalitarianism. Inspired by the testimony of Whittaker Chambers (1901–1961), the second group was the anticommunists, many of its members being defectors from socialism. They devoted themselves to vehemently fighting the threat posed by this enemy, both abroad—the Soviet Union and its allies—and within American society, where they detected infiltration by agents and sympathizers of Soviet communism in the media, in the arts, and even in the government. Finally, the cultural conservatives, or traditionalists, whose view was artic-

---

7. George H Nash, *The Conservative Intellectual Movement in America: Since 1945*, 2nd ed. (ISI Books, 1996).

ulated in Russell Kirk's *The Conservative Mind*, emphasized more clearly the importance of both the moral and cultural traditions derived from classical Greco-Roman and Judeo-Christian cultures and the British legacy, alongside the specific bases that forged the United States' nationality in its formation during the colonial and independence periods.

In the Brazilian environment, from the 1930s onward, the situation was far worse. The agenda regarding the government's growth as a promoter of development was equally triumphant, even more emphatically so, but, due to the dictatorial regime of the so-called New State, established in 1937 by Getúlio Vargas (1882-1954) under the pretext of protecting Brazil against communism and other amorphous perils, which reinforced all the patrimonial aspects of the national political culture. Having dismantled and persecuted all the forces that stood for freedom, he built a political machinery that would survive until the end of the regime and keep Vargas's allies in power in the future. As a Germanophile authoritarian, Vargas, in theory, was more sympathetic during World War II toward the Axis, but, in coordination with Roosevelt, as well as due to the protests of Brazilian civil society, he placed Brazil alongside the Allies, even sending Brazilian troops to fight with Americans in the Italian military campaign.

Despite being a nationalist and supporter of Varguism, diplomat Osvaldo Aranha (1894–1960), who was Minister of Foreign Affairs from 1938 to 1944, is worth mentioning here as a protagonist in the effort to position Brazil by the side of the democratic West and the United States. He presided, moreover, at the UN session which, in 1947, assured the creation of the State of Israel. In his analysis of the ideology of Varguism, diplomat and political scientist José Osvaldo de Meira Penna stated that "Vargas has always seemed inconsistent," adding that the dictator "was deliberately inconsistent and well-aware of it," acting "with supreme expertise and cynicism."[8]

After the end of World War II, when Vargas's dictatorship officially came to an end, the 1946 Constitution inaugurated a multiparty system, in which three parties stood out: aside from the aforementioned UDN (National Democratic Union), which brought together different opposition forces, there were the PSD (*Partido Social Democrático*; Social Democratic Party) and the PTB (*Partido Trabalhista Brasileiro*; Brazilian Labor Party), which did nothing more than reconstitute the electoral disputes that had characterized the formally extinguished Vargas dictatorship.

As suggested by the motto "the cost of freedom is eternal vigilance," liberal forces were concentrated around the UDN's project, although the degree of pro-market and pro-liberty convictions within the party was quite variable, for what truly unified the association was the opposition to Varguism—and even there, the intensity of the opposition was not uniform. From the ex-

---

8. José Osvaldo de Meira Penna, *A Ideologia do Século XX: Ensaios sobre o Nacional-socialismo, o Marxismo, o Terceiro-mundismo e a Ideologia Brasileira*, 2nd ed. (Nórdica, 1994), 152.

tinction of the empire in 1889 until that time, Brazil had had no less than four distinct republican constitutions—implemented, respectively, in 1891, 1932, 1937, and 1946—and had also maintained, unlike the monarchic regime supported by the 1824 Constitution, relatively fragile institutions that coexisted with institutional subversions and military coups, which lasted from 1946 to 1964, when an ultimate act of force imposed a military regime. Throughout that period, most of the governments were ruled by figures associated, in greater or lesser degree, with Varguism. The only exception was President Jânio Quadros (1917–1992), who, during his brief time in the government in 1961—less than eight months ending in a surprising resignation—established a foreign policy with independent pretenses, having come to honor communist leader Che Guevara (1928–1967), not to mention his populist character and his conflicts with the parliament. The first president of that period, Eurico Gaspar Dutra (1883–1974), despite having been a Germanophile and supporter of the Vargas dictatorship, was staunchly anticommunist, and, with the advent of the Cold War, he aligned Brazilian foreign policy with that of the United States. In general, the remaining governments between 1946 and 1964 oscillated between nationalist and anti-American populist rhetoric, on one hand, and on the other hand, pragmatic deals meant to get Washington's support for national developmentalist policies. The second government of this epoch, 1951 to 1954, was presided over by Vargas, who this time returned to power by popular vote. However, facing accusations of corruption, he ended up committing suicide.

The most popular leader of the UDN back then, as well as the fiercest opponent of Varguism, was journalist Carlos Lacerda (1914–1977), a former communist deeply influenced by the American Catholic anticommunist Archbishop Fulton Sheen (1895–1979), by the activism of fellow countryman Rui Barbosa, by Winston Churchill's (1874–1965) British conservative tendencies, and by Konrad Adenauer's (1876–1967) German Christian democracy, as well as by the economic positions of the so-called German social market economy, proposed by Ludwig Erhard (1897–1977). Always fundamentally concerned with Brazil's own national interests, Lacerda was viscerally opposed to the Soviet Union and defended the importance of Brazil's friendship with the United States, in what he deemed to be a confrontation between civilizations and values. His wish was to unite the American continent and ward off the rhetoric and political power held by anti-Americanist forces, which made a lot of noise among socialists, communists, and "right-wing nationalists" in Latin America, a phenomenon that also affected Brazil. According to Lacerda,

> Our unity depends on the integration of a system which one might call intra-American. A rising rhythm, a philosophy that spreads with a certain and defined attitude regarding life, that is what we have in common. . . . Individualism is not a privilege of Anglo-Saxon culture. On that score, we are just as old as they are. We have been individualists since the Old Testament, since Greece and Rome. The individu-

alism of the Reformation, of the Bible as interpreted, is not greater than the one of the Counter-Reformation, of the Bible as revealed. . . . Why not channel individualism as a creative force, and, with it, organize a democratic society? . . . What is missing for us to perform a great work of continental integration is the act of restoring, these days, the faith with which those ideals were defended by our greatest men, in each of our countries. And to carry out, in our days, before the danger posed by the disunity of the Americas and the destruction of the world, a work of worldwide repercussion: the integration of the American continent in favor of the progress of its peoples. Only when everyone feels that each of our problems affects all of us will it be possible to provide to each of our solutions everyone's cooperation. When the Latin American peoples objectively feel that the North American people is fraternally by their side, there will be no communism capable of stopping, in each of those peoples, that voice of the earth and the blood, that appeal of history, that continental reality, that survival instinct which will lead to the ever-growing unity of this part of the world, as the greatest contribution it can make to progress and to peace in its land and in the rest of the world as well.[9]

Analogously, the agenda for the liberal and conservative movement in Brazil is anti-Vargasian, much like the libertarian and conservative agenda in the United States is anti-Rooseveltian. However, the military regime implemented in 1964, even though it took, during the first presidential government, presided over by Marshal Humberto Castelo Branco (1897–1967), a stand that was opposed to Varguism, over time, under the pretext of fighting the extreme left and corruption, ended up destroying the UDN's liberal anti-Vargasian basis. This program was replaced, during that administration and those of the succeeding four military presidents (1967–1985), by an increasingly interventionist approach, with the multiplication of state-owned companies and grandiose public works. In that sense, one might posit an analogy between the Brazilian authoritarian epoch and the "Great Society" reforms of American President Lyndon Johnson (1908–1973), approximately at the same time, which updated the New Deal's interventionist agenda, just as the Brazilian military regimes undertook a new version of Vargas's bureaucratic management.

In the 1980s, politics in the United States went through the so-called Reagan Era, marked by the reaffirmation of the anticommunist posture in foreign affairs and by the internal adoption of

---

9. Carlos Lacerda, *O Poder das Ideias* (Record, 1963), 236-241.

administrative measures favorable to economic freedom and the limitation of state interventionism. In quite a distinct way, the first year of the so-called Brazilian New Republic, a period which in 1985, succeeded the military governments, was characterized by a continuing fondness for the Vargas model, which provided reason for the 1980s to be known as "the lost decade." The worst legacy of that time in Brazil, however, was the one left by the 1988 Constitution, which, besides maintaining or broadening many elements of both the patrimonial heritage and the models of developmentalist interventionism typical of the Vargas Era and the military regimes, also generated legal insecurity, political instability, and economic stagnation.

In defense of economic freedom, through the last decades of the twentieth century an emerging generation of Brazilian liberals—who will be further analyzed in this work's conclusion—strongly criticized the errors of the new Constitutional Charter, in particular, and more broadly, the ills of interventionist policies. Within this liberal rebirth, two names worth noting are the diplomat and parliamentarian Roberto Campos (1917–2001) and the entrepreneur Henry Maksoud (1929–2014), both influenced by Hayekian thinking. It is also worth pointing out the actions of Canada-born entrepreneur Donald Stewart Jr. (1931–1999), who in 1983 captained the foundation of the *Instituto Liberal* (IL, Liberal Institute), molded in the likeness of American think tanks, which gathered Brazilian intellectuals, spread the ideas of foreign authors, and developed policy papers.

From the mid-1990s, the country underwent important reforms enhancing the flexibility of the market, substantial privatizations, and fiscal adjustments, yet the period was marked by the ideological prevalence of social democracy. At the beginning of the twenty-first century, after having been, throughout three decades, the main left-wing force of opposition to all the previous governments, the PT (*Partido dos Trabalhadores*; Labor Party) finally came into power, holding the presidency of Brazil uninterruptedly for over thirteen years, from 2003 from 2016. During the first year of President Luís Inácio "Lula" da Silva's administration, several of the policies that had been implemented during the social democratic administration of Fernando Henrique Cardoso (1995–2003) were preserved; however, the new socialist government gradually imposed its progressive ideological agenda and increased state intervention, especially in the economy—besides establishing the largest corruption scheme in Brazilian history. The immeasurable dissatisfaction of the Brazilian people, who took to the streets to protest against the government, combined with an inability to maintain political coalitions as well as the economic crisis, provoked the 2016 impeachment of President Dilma Roussef, legally carried out by the House of Representatives and the Senate, removing her from office.

Within this context of opposition to the federal administration of the PT, the so-called "New Right" arose, constituted by different groups, many antagonistic toward one another. Among the varied segments of the New Right, four main strands may be distinguished. The first one is, first and foremost, linked to the anti-corruption cause, a problem that is perennially widespread in Brazilian public life and which was made explicit by the scandals exposed by the judicial investigation known as Operation Car Wash during the last years of Dilma's government. A second element, closer to conservative ideals, is mainly composed of Christians, both Evangelicals and Catholics, and focuses on defending religious, family, and patriotic principles. There are also libertarian factions, characterized by the defense of economic freedom against state interventionism. Finally, there are ever-decreasing numbers of people who, taking a vehemently anticommunist stand, advocate military intervention to free the nation from the red menace. As will be discussed in the conclusion, the first three strands represent a growing constituency who, once fed with the right ideas, can help turn Brazil into a virtuous, prosperous, free society.

Conclusion

The New Right's political and intellectual movement may seem like a massive, irreversible force in Brazil, as, through social media, it reaches an ever-growing number of people. According to a survey recently released by the newspaper *O Estado de São Paulo*, 41 percent of Brazilian voters consider themselves to be right-wing, whereas only 28 percent claim they're centrists, merely 18 percent are left-wingers, and the remaining 13 percent either don't know where they stand or didn't want to provide an answer. Undoubtedly, Brazilian citizens' greater clarity regarding their electoral preferences, in lieu of mere compliance with populist leaders, is in a symbiotic way related to the opposition movements to the PT (*Partido dos Trabalhadores*; Labor Party), which from 2013 onward brought millions of people to the streets to protest, not only against the blatant corruption but also against various progressive and socialist agendas. Nonetheless, the current emergence of the New Right, being more than just a circumstantial revolt aimed at a specific government, reflects the hard work of a group of intellectuals and institutions that sowed the soil in which opposition to dominant leftism flourished.

Four important twentieth-century Brazilian intellectuals who developed theoretical elaborations of conservative or classical liberal tendencies, making use of American bibliographic references, have been mentioned in previous chapters: João Camilo de Oliveira Torres, Gilberto Freyre, José Osvaldo de Meira Penna, and Antonio Paim.

As a notable historian of political ideas, with an emphasis on the imperial epoch, João Camilo de Oliveira Torres produced extensive studies on the liberal experience in Brazil throughout the nineteenth century, on the monarchic Conservative Party, on the country's federalist ideas with respect to positivist doctrine, and on Brazilian presidentialism. In his conservative approach, he was an avowed follower of the thought of Russell Kirk, whose famous six canons he used in his 1968 book *Os Construtores do Império* (The Builders of the Empire), where he treated the Brazilian conservative movement. Based on Kirk's conceptualization, Oliveira Torres defined conservatism as "a political position that acknowledges that the existence of communities is subjected to certain conditions, and that social changes, in order to be just and valid, cannot disrupt the continuity between the past and the future."[1]

---

1. João Camilo de Oliveira Torres, *Os Construtores do Império* (Edições Câmara, 2017), 21.

CONCLUSION

Polymath Gilberto Freyre was a versatile thinker who not only developed a study on Brazil's material and intellectual historical aspects, but also committed himself to unveiling the Brazilian soul. It is worth noting that such an illustrious man, author of extensive sociological, historical, anthropological, and literary work, was a member of the UDN, through which he was elected a congressman, and on several occasions defined himself as a conservative. The general thesis defended by Freyre in his classic *The Masters and the Slaves* is that the relationships between Portuguese Caucasians, Native Americans, and black-skinned Africans, the three main groups that constituted Brazil, were consolidated through landowner monoculture, thence giving rise to a patriarchal social organization which forged Brazilian nationality (see chapter 2 above).[2] Along with reading the myriad works by H. L. Mencken (1880–1956) and the literary scholars known as the Southern Agrarians, among other American authors, the Brazilian anthropologist's experience at Baylor University provided him with the ability to compare another society rooted in slavery, landowner-ship, and patriarchy with the Brazilian situation, which allowed

---

2. Gilberto Freyre, *The Masters and the Slaves: A Study in the Development of Brazilian Civilization* (Alfred A. Knopf, 1946).

him to more directly assess the similarities and differences between them.³ According to João Camilo de Oliveira Torres, the Freyrean mentality "established, within several of his works, that Portugal had adopted a 'Christocentric' rather than 'ethnocentric' concept of colonization," given that "the racial differences disappeared before the unity of faith."⁴ As in the case of Russell Kirk, there lies, in the works of Gilberto Freyre, a debt to American poet T. S. Eliot, whose notion of a Christian society has served as a methodological basis for understanding "the amplitude of Christianity as an immense cultural park, to which Brazil belongs as a result of the effort of Portuguese colonization."⁵

Besides knowing the works of Russell Kirk as well, diplomat and political scientist José Osvaldo de Meira Penna was a forceful advocate of Burkean, Tocquevillian, and Hayekian theses. A member of the Mont Pèlerin Society who lived to be over a hundred years old, he left a vast corpus in the fields of social psycholo-

---

3. A general analysis of the Freyrean thinking, as well as the illustrious Brazilian author's biography, is presented in Peter Burke and Maria Lúcia G. Pallares-Burke, *Gilberto Freyre: Social Theory in the Tropics* (Peter Lang, 2008).

4. João Camilo de Oliveira Torres, *Interpretação da Realidade Brasileira* (Edições Câmara, 2017), 254.

5. Gilberto Freyre, *Uma Cultura Ameaçada e Outros Ensaios* (É Realizações, 2010), 54.

gy, political theory, and public ethics, in which he elaborated on the religious, moral, psychological, sociological, cultural, political, economic, and ideological aspects of the Brazilian delay in economic development in comparison to other nations. In addition to his writings on Brazilian social psychology and the twentieth century's ideologies, mentioned respectively in the second and fourth chapters of this book, Meira Penna developed both an in-depth study on the phenomenon of patrimonialism, which plagues Brazil,[6] and a broad discussion of modern revolutions, in which he compared the British, North American, and Brazilian cases, emphasizing the positive legacy bequeathed by classical liberalism and socialist deviations in these experiences.[7] Among the author's extensive bibliography, it is worth highlighting his criticism of liberation theology, which was influenced by his friend Michael Novak (1933–2017), whose writings revealed the Marxist features of liberation theology's misrepresentation of the Christ-

---

6. José Osvaldo de Meira Penna, *O Dinossauro: Uma Pesquisa sobre o Estado, o Patrimonialismo Selvagem e a Nova Classe de Intelectuais e Burocratas* (T. A. Queiroz, 1988).

7. José Osvaldo de Meira Penna, *O Espírito das Revoluções: Da Revolução Gloriosa à Revolução Liberal*, 2nd ed. (VIDE Editorial, 2016).

ian message, which turned the "preferential option for the poor" into a preferential option for poverty.[8]

Finally, there are the valuable contributions made by Antonio Paim, who over the course of more than five decades spent producing his vast bibliography, took part in political activities, created postgraduate courses, and elaborated crucial philosophical and historical analyses, with a special emphasis on Brazilian thought and liberalism. Besides Kirkian conservatism, the Brazilian thinker also discussed the relevance of the liberal or conservative proposals presented by John Dewey (1859–1952), Mortimer J. Adler (1902–2001), Robert A. Nisbet (1913–1996), Robert A. Dahl (1915–2014), Irving Kristol (1920–2009), John Rawls (1921–2002), Samuel P. Huntington (1927–2008), and Robert Nozick (1938–2002), among other American authors analyzed in his various works.[9]

It should be pointed out that Paim and Meira Penna, although the former was more inclined to social liberalism and the latter to conservatism, remained friends for over four decades, both joining efforts in several initiatives that included other relevant Brazilian authors. Among the intellectuals who were part of the group that revolved around those two thinkers, it is worth noting

---

8. José Osvaldo de Meira Penna, *Opção Preferencial pela Riqueza* (Instituto Liberal, 1991).

9. See Antonio Paim, *O Liberalismo Contemporâneo*, 2nd ed. (Tempo Brasileiro, 2000).

the philosopher, historian, and jurist Ubiratan Borges de Macedo (1937–2007), who, between the years 1980 and 1982, when he acted as a Brazilian attaché in the Organization of American States (OAS) in Washington, DC, and as a professor in the Inter-American Defense College (IADC), maintained contact with the works of several American classical liberal and conservative authors, whose words he helped spread in Brazil. Apart from Kirkian thinking, he also assessed the body of work of conservative Willmoore Kendall (1909–1967) and the debate over the so-called Theory of Justice in its many threads, including Hayekian criticisms. It is worth mentioning, among his writings, a book on the ideal of freedom in Brazil during the empire, in which he stressed the importance of French doctrinal liberalism for Brazilian conservatism, and also made a pioneering distinction between Brazilian conservative ideas, inspired by the British parliamentary experience, and political traditionalism, oriented by French ultramontane views, in addition differentiating the latter from philosophical traditionalism. Moreover, in the same work, he reflected on the Brazilian Catholic mindset during this period.[10] Yet, his most well-known writing is a volume in which he discussed the issues of classical liberalism and social justice, dedicating a whole chapter to analysis of Michael Novak's "democratic capitalism" thesis—thus emphasizing the importance of such a proposal as

---

10. Ubiratan Borges de Macedo, *A Ideia de Liberdade no Século XIX: O Caso Brasileiro*, 2nd ed. (Expressão e Cultura, 1998).

a necessary means to assure the viability of the market economy, guided by classical liberal principles and associated with Christian values, which enable a free, virtuous society.[11]

Regardless of the great contribution made by such illustrious thinkers, the main impulse toward the dissemination in Brazil of the writings of authors who were affiliated with theoretical and political streams—hitherto unusual in the country—such as the Austrian school of economics, derives from the breakthrough initiative taken by the *Instituto Liberal*, founded, on January 16, 1983, in the city of Rio de Janeiro, by the previously mentioned engineer and entrepreneur Donald Stewart Jr.. The main inspiration behind the creation of this Brazilian think tank was the experience of the British Institute of Economic Affairs (IEA). However, IL maintained relationships, through its founder, with diverse American institutions, such as the Foundation for Economic Education (FEE), the American Enterprise Institute (AEI), the Heritage Foundation, the Cato Institute, the Atlas Network, Liberty Fund, and the Acton Institute, which, over IL's forty-plus years of existence, were maintained and broadened by its successive leaders. Throughout its four decades of operation, the IL was responsible for translating and editing books, carrying out colloquiums, and gathering together Brazilian intellectuals who were dedicated to

---

11. Ubiratan Borges de Macedo, "O Espírito do Capitalismo Democrático," in *Liberalismo e Justiça Social* (IBRASA, 1995), 69-73.

the support of a society based on order and freedom. Furthermore, it is noteworthy that the aforementioned scholars José Osvaldo de Meira Penna, Antonio Paim, and Ubiratan Borges de Macedo were regular collaborators of the institute, offering lectures, writing countless texts, and taking part in debates in the various colloquiums.

IL's main scholarly anchor was Professor Og Francisco Leme (1922–2004), given that he was responsible both for bringing together a number of Brazilian intellectuals in the work of the institute and for developing the academic programs geared toward the solid education of the youth. After finishing law school, followed by the sociology program in the University of São Paulo, where he was a pupil of American sociologist Donald Pierson (1900–1995), Leme decided, following Pierson's advice, to study economics at the University of Chicago University. There, during the 1950s, he had as mentors such eminent figures as Frank H. Knight (1885–1972), F. A. Hayek (1899–1992), Theodore Schultz (1902–1998), George J. Stigler (1911–1991), Milton Friedman (1912–2006), and H. Gregg Lewis (1914–1992).

The success of IL served as a model for countless other organizations and individuals throughout Brazil, who comprised a wide network dedicated to the diffusion of the principles of individual liberty, the rule of law, the free market economy, and representative democracy. This network especially gained strength during the crisis of PT's government when, enabled by technology and social media, it helped spur the emergence of the New Right. The American influence over the rising Brazilian right is explicit, both respect to both its intellectual influences and the groups into which it divided itself—creating divisions and factions similar to those within the conservative movement in the United States.

Long before a substantial portion of the Brazilian population awakened to the ills of leftism—not only the most radical strand represented by PT and its allies but also its moderate social-democratic version, embraced since the beginning of the 1980s by most political associations—several institutions, apart from IL, advocated the importance of individual liberties and the institutions that made them possible. The *Instituto de Estudos Empresariais* (IEE, Brazilian Institute of Entrepreneurial Studies) was founded in 1984, in Porto Alegre in the state of Rio Grande do Sul, as a center for the formation of leaders between the ages of twenty and thirty-two years old. Based on the principles of freedom and individual responsibilities, as well as the defense of the rule of law and private property, the IEE was responsible for graduating over a thousand businessmen over the course of its forty years of existence. Aside from its ongoing program of formation of new leadership, the IEE has sponsored annually, for thirty-seven years now, the Forum of Liberty, an initiative that has reached over eighty-five thousand people since 1988. A number of renowned North American intellectuals have participated over the years as speakers, among them economists James M. Buchanan (1919–2013), Douglass North (1920–2015), Gary Becker (1930–2014), Israel Kirzner (1930–), and Walter E. Williams (1936–2020); historian Richard Pipes (1923–2018); political scientist Charles A. Murray (1943–); and Father Robert A. Sirico (1951–).

Inspired by the example given by the American Mises Institute and by the IL's experience, Brazilian engineer and businessman Helio Beltrão, who got his MBA from Columbia University in New York, founded in 2007 the *Instituto Mises Brasil* (IMB), which is currently the nation's main institutional proponent of the thought of the Austrian school. Aside from maintaining three postgraduate programs and an academic magazine, it edits books, has a large social media presence, runs a popular weekly podcast (with over five hundred episodes), and publishes daily articles on its website.

Having served in IL since the 1980s, Brazilian businessman Salim Mattar, inspired by the IEE model, founded in 2007 in Belo Horizonte the *Instituto de Formação de Líderes* (IFL, Institute for Formation of Leaders), which over the past seventeen years has opened a total of thirteen additional independent branches in the cities of São Paulo, Campinas, Rio de Janeiro, Brasília, Curitiba, Florianópolis, Goiânia, Recife, Salvador, Gramado, and Lajeado, besides maintaining in Belo Horizonte and São Paulo similar institutions for youths between the ages of sixteen and twenty-two. Through almost two decades, the fourteen IFLs, most of them created recently, have graduated a total of 1,350 people and currently count 667 associates who take part in the cycle of formation. Much like the Forum of Liberty sponsored by IEE in the city of Porto Alegre, IFL's affiliates in the cities of Belo Horizonte, São Paulo, Curitiba, and Florianópolis organize great annual events in their respective capitals, which thousands of people have already attended, with the audience increasing every year, and many of them featuring renowned North American speakers.

Affiliated with the North American organization Students for Liberty (SFL) since its foundation in 2012, Students for Liberty Brazil (SFLB) is a crucial pillar in the country's classical liberal and conservative movement. Over the past twelve years of continuous operation, the organization has formed over five thousand college students and organized an annual national event and several statewide conferences, in addition to encouraging the work of other student organizations. Today, SFLB has a network of 325 active volunteers throughout Brazil, associated with local chapters that are present in the federal district and in twenty-three of the twenty-six states that constitute the Brazilian federation.

Like the conservative movement in the United States, which, according to George Nash, is a coalition of three groups (see chapter 4 above), in Brazil the New Right phenomenon also encompasses distinct factions, some of which are quite similar to their North American counterparts. In the current intellectual and political climate in Brazil, classical liberals and libertarians, mostly influenced by the Austrian or Chicago schools of economics, are represented in the nation by quite varied groups. Among these are some aligned with the anarcho-capitalist tradition, disciples of Murray Rothbard (1926–1995), who collaborate on great events and various projects, which are especially popular among the youth. Anticommunism also stridently manifests itself on the Brazilian right, though it is more diffusely present, lacking the organizations of which classical liberals and conservatives boast but ever-present in the mindset of many who fight against progressive and socialist agendas. Endowed with larger philosophical and historical bases, in spite of the absence of effectives think thanks, there is also a Brazilian element which, in many aspects, is similar to North American cultural conservativism: it emphasizes the importance of the pillars of Western civilization, including a free-market economy that is linked to moral values and traditional institutions.

These features of the Brazilian situation do not represent any great novelty. If a historical stroll through the Brazilian experience in comparison with the United States teaches anything, it is that, despite its obvious particularities, Brazil has always considered itself a part of the Christian-culture-based Western world, contrary to what most foreign interpreters erroneously argue. Even when there weren't many Brazilians praising their European, monarchic roots, there were those who emphasized their American aspirations for liberty.

The seductive attempt of a simple transposition of American institutions, however, is unfeasible due to undeniable Brazilian particularities. Among these, we highlight the greater activism of the state in public life, inherited from the experience of the Portuguese monarchy. This factor must be considered by all those who, guided by conservative classical liberal principles, wish to nudge the country toward the path of freedom and prosperity. Advocates of liberty in Brazil must aspire to occupy public positions so as to effect the changes the nation so desperately needs.

The New Right phenomenon has brought about greater involvement of conservative and classical liberal leaders with partisan politics—as occurred during the empire, when intellectuals from earlier generations likewise disdained such activity. Besides the fact that a sizable number of citizens have woken up from the political apathy characteristic of the Republican period, countless politicians in Brazil nowadays have embraced the labels "conservative" and "liberal" (in the classical sense). Although, in truth, many of them should not be classified as such, the popularity of such terms shows a promising tendency within the electoral market of Brazilian politics.

In that connection, it is worth stressing a specific commendable parliamentary experience. In 2020, the *Frente Parlamentar do Livre Mercado* (FPLM, Parliamentary Front for the Free Market) was created, its main goal being to make sure that Brazil advances ten positions in the Index of Economic Freedom by the year 2026, through legislative actions that inhibit state intervention and broaden economic freedom. Among the 513 federal congressmen of the current legislature, initiated in 2023, FPLM counts on the participation of 187 signatories, representatives within the lower house of twenty-six of the twenty-seven federative units and affiliated with eighteen distinct political parties. The FPLM also includes twenty-seven senators among the eighty-one who constitute the higher house. The work done by congressmen and senators who belong to FPLM is supported by the Instituto Livre Mercado (ILM, Free Market Institute), a think tank financed exclusively by private funds, which advises parliamentarians on specific legislation, aside from proposing laws that support a business environment characterized by a greater economic freedom and legal security.

Despite the adversities and difficulties Brazil has faced, both with the return of the PT to power in 2023 and with the abuses of authority committed by ministries of the Supreme Court, the country's current status is much different from the bleak 2003 situation, when Lula first ascended to power. The difference between the two periods may be best explained by a fable written by eminent Brazilian writer José Bento Monteiro Lobato (1882–1948), a notable opponent of Varguism and great admirer of the United States:

> Two donkeys roamed about, one of them carried sugar, the other sponges.

> The first one said, "Let's tread carefully, as the road is dangerous."

> The other one argued, "Dangerous how? We could simply follow the tracks left by those who were walking here today before us."

"It doesn't always work that way. Where one has passed, another one might not."

"What a stupid thing to say! I know how to live and brag about it, and my whole knowledge comes down to merely imitating what others do."

"It doesn't always work that way," the first donkey persisted.

Soon thereafter they got to the river, whose bridge had fallen the day before.

"Now what?" said the first.

"Let's just cross the river," replied the other.

The donkey carrying sugar entered the stream and, as his cargo dissolved upon coming into contact with the water, he quickly got to the other side.

The donkey carrying the sponges, true to his ideas, thought to himself, "Well, if he pulled through it, then so will I."

So he got into the river—except that his cargo, instead of dissolving, absorbed the water, and its weight increased to a point where the poor fool plunged straight to the bottom.

> The moral of the story is, "Do not imitate others."[12]

In certain cases, it is unwise to imitate even one's own past actions, without first comprehending the contextual changes undergone or, as imperial conservatives would say, without recognizing "the primacy of circumstance." Given the international economic situation and the internal political situation in 2003, one might say that Lula, in his first presidential term, was crossing a river carrying sugar, whereas, during his current and third term, he is carrying sponges. In less than two decades, Brazil underwent significant changes which, besides the rise of a vigorous political opposition to leftist ideals, have also created, within the cultural, religious, and economic environments, a scenario that is propitious to the evolution of ideas in favor of freedom.

Throughout the past twenty years, IL's pioneering commitment in the 1980s and 1990s to providing in Portuguese works by authors who disagreed with the leftist consensus reverberated through the publishing market, which is now receptive to producing the writings of various Brazilian and foreign authors of

---

12. Monteiro Lobato, "Serões de Dona Benta e História das Invenções," in *Obras Completas de Monteiro Lobato – Literatura Infantil*, vol. 8, 2nd series São Paulo: (Editora Brasiliense Ltda., 1956).

conservative or libertarian tendencies. Social networks allowed for a broader circulation of ideas, which facilitated the spread of classical liberalism and conservatism and, moreover, mobilized voluntary right-wing activism. It should also be pointed out that, thanks to a law passed in 2016, the nefarious compulsory union tax implemented by Getúlio Vargas, was abolished, thus making the contribution to unions optional, a factor which deprived leftist activism of millions of dollars of financing. Despite the apparent hegemony of liberation theology among the members of the episcopate, a great many Catholic believers, including many young priests, have been moving in a conservative direction. Another key factor for the emergence of the New Right was the rise of Protestant Evangelicalism, which has converted millions of Brazilians. Finally, in economic terms, it is noteworthy that Brazil has been experiencing impressive growth, especially within its Central-West, where agribusiness thrives, an example of productivity for the rest of the world.

This new Brazil, both in the realm of ideas and in the economic field, deserves special attention from the North American people. Contrasting the *bandeirantes* in Brazil with the pioneers in the United States, the aforementioned Clodomir Viana Moog predicted that the latest wave of European immigrants could counterbalance the vice of *bandeirante* psychology regarding labor. He expected there to occur "a last consequence stemming from the arrival of German, Italian, and Portuguese colonists in couples, families, communities: the modification of the Brazilian mentality in the sense of developing its spirit of association and its economic virtues."[13]

Nowadays, there are, indeed, immense potential and plentiful resources to be explored in Brazil, both within the economic sphere and in the market of ideas. Greater collaboration between Brazilians and Americans in combating progressive and socialist ideologies is paramount. Such harmful ideas endanger the lush tree of the West, which may come to rot, since the agents of such perversions in both countries have not only been cooperating with one another but also incessantly exchanging ideas and resources. There is still a margin for the diverse existing connections between the two nations to be put to good use, thus making it possible, in the near future, to generate healthier seeds.

The two giants of the New World have, in their favor, an air filled with youth and diversity, but also the heavy responsibility to preserve an old message, a noble common heritage, which both have the potential to carry and unfurl. Now it's up to the descendants of *bandeirantes* and pioneers, upon mutually enlightening themselves and each other with their qualities and experiences, to decide whether they'll accept such a vital call and fight together in the battle for free, virtuous, and thriving societies.

---

13. Clodomir Viana Moog, *Bandeirantes e Pioneiros: Paralelo entre duas culturas* (Editora Globo, 1957), 334.

www.ingramcontent.com/pod-product-compliance
Lightning Source LLC
LaVergne TN
LVHW010330070526
838199LV00065B/5708